# ECONOMIES
## OF THE
## WORLD TODAY

### THIRD EDITION

THIRD EDITION

# ECONOMIES OF THE WORLD TODAY

## THEIR ORGANIZATION, DEVELOPMENT, AND PERFORMANCE

**CLAIR WILCOX**
late of Swarthmore College

**WILLIS D. WEATHERFORD, JR.**
Berea College

**HOLLAND HUNTER**
Haverford College

**MORTON S. BARATZ**
University of Maryland

HARCOURT BRACE JOVANOVICH, INC.

New York      Chicago      San Francisco      Atlanta

ISBN: 0-15-519717-7

Library of Congress Catalog Card Number: 75-42900

Printed in the United States of America

# PREFACE

*Economies of the World Today* was brought into being because its authors were convinced that the introductory course in economics should culminate in an orderly scrutiny of several different economies. We felt that students would thus obtain a clearer perspective on their own economy, that the principles and problems they had studied would take on a new significance when viewed in relation to economies of different kinds. We found, however, that the teaching materials available were inadequate for this purpose. The discussion of comparative economies in the introductory texts was too brief; the discussion in the advanced texts was too long. The success of our first two editions has shown that a compact treatment indeed fills a need. It has also proved usable as an independent text.

*Economies of the World Today* does not concern itself with doctrinal history, directing the student's attention, instead, to what is actually happening today. We ask how economies are organized—looking at individualism and collectivism, market economies and centrally directed economies. We examine the process of economic development looking all the way from economies just beginning the process to one that is pushing beyond economic maturity. We review interacting growth rates of output and population—asking why some economies have been raising per capita output rapidly and others slowly. We inquire, finally, into the quality of each economy's performance. Within this broad framework we survey the economies of three comparatively low-income countries: China, India, and Mexico; and three relatively high-income areas: the USSR, the European Community, and the United States.

We chose these economies for several reasons. First, they are large and important. Second, they display great diversity in institutional structure. Third, they illustrate several ways of dealing with the difficult problems of regional coordination that are often overlooked in introductory texts. The European Community is a loose grouping of nine separate nation-states; how does its economic management differ from, say, that of China's 26 provinces or India's 20 constituent states?

The late Clair Wilcox organized the first edition and wrote its first and last chapters. President Willis Weatherford of Berea College wrote the original chapter on India; those on the USSR and

**v**

China were written by Holland Hunter. Wilcox and Weatherford were too busy to work on the second edition; so with their advice and consent, updating and revising were carried out by Hunter and Professor Morton S. Baratz. For the third edition, Baratz has written new chapters on Mexico and the European Community and has shared in revising the other five. We appreciate helpful criticism from Elizabeth Clayton, Nicolas Spulber, and Elias Tuma; expert editorial guidance from Josephine Satloff and Gail Lemkowitz; and magnificent secretarial support from Adeline Taraborelli and Pam (Gagnon) Greeff. While all chapters have benefited from this help, traces of individual stubbornness remain. This, we hope, is the strength of a pluralist enterprise.

H. H.
M. S. B.

# CONTENTS

# 1

## THE WORLD'S ECONOMIES    1

Forms of economic organization
The process of economic development
Growth rates of output and population
Standards of economic performance

# 2

## CHINA    32

A new command economy,
driving toward development, growing in spurts

# 3

## INDIA    59

An old market economy,
striving toward development, growing painfully

# 4

## MEXICO    88

A youthful market economy,
midway in development, growing vigorously

# 5

## THE SOVIET UNION    110

An old command economy,
not yet mature, growing lopsidedly

# 6

## THE EUROPEAN ECONOMIC COMMUNITY    134

A new market-economy grouping,
mostly mature, growing steadily

# 7

## UNITED STATES OF AMERICA    158

An old market economy,
pushing past maturity, growing in new ways

# ECONOMIES
## OF THE
## WORLD TODAY

### THIRD EDITION

# THE WORLD'S ECONOMIES

The economies of the world today differ from one another in many respects. They differ most importantly in their form of economic organization, in their stage of economic development, and in their rate of economic growth. In some nations economic initiative is largely left to the individual and economic activity is coordinated through the market; in others initiative is taken and activity is coordinated by the government. Some economies are in the early stages of industrialization, some are advanced industrially, and at least one is "post-industrial" in character. Some are stagnant, others growing. It is our purpose to explore the factors that underlie these differences.

In the following chapters we shall examine in some detail the structure and performance of six economies—China, India, Mexico, the Soviet Union, the European Community, and the United States. In this chapter we define the forms of economic organization, the process of economic development, and the rates of economic growth, classifying the economies of the world in accordance with these definitions. We also discuss the standards by which the performance of an economy may be appraised: does it produce plenty, does it permit freedom of choice, does it provide equal opportunities, does it run smoothly, does it grow?

## FORMS OF ECONOMIC ORGANIZATION

The forms of economic organization are usually labeled capitalism on the one hand and socialism or communism on the other. Since the meaning of these words is ambiguous, we shall dispose of them at the outset. And since communists assert that their system embodies the economic theories of Karl Marx, we pause briefly to consider these theories. We then proceed to define the concepts of economic individualism and economic collectivism and to distinguish between controlled economies and market economies.

**The ambiguity of capitalism, socialism, communism**    The word *capital* has many meanings. Customarily, it means producers' goods—plant and equipment that do not themselves satisfy consumers' wants but are used in producing other goods. An economy may be said to be *capitalistic* if its technology requires the employment of large amounts of capital. In this sense the U.S. economy and the Soviet economy are both capitalistic. *Capitalism* is usually applied, however, to economies in which most producers' goods are privately owned. In this sense the U.S. economy is capitalistic, and the Soviet economy is not.

*Socialism* is often defined as the public ownership of producers' goods and *communism* as the public ownership of most wealth, including both producers' and consumers' goods. Socialism was once regarded as an earlier stage in the evolution of communism. But establishment of communism has come to be associated with drastic, often violent, change and with totalitarian government; socialism with peaceful change and democratic government. The meanings of *socialism* and *communism* are obscured, too, because opponents of specific economic reforms in capitalistic economies usually denounce them as socialistic or communistic even though the reforms involve no extension of public ownership.

Not only are these words ambiguous; they fail, as we shall see, to reveal the more significant differences between the forms of economic organization. And they are charged with emotion, each being used more often to condemn than to describe. We shall therefore abandon them in favor of terms that are more concrete and less colored.

**The limited relevance of Marxism**    Karl Marx, a German philosopher who lived from 1818 to 1883, was both a political agitator and a serious scholar. His lifework, *Das Kapital*, or *Capital*, became the bible of communism. He did not attempt in his book to tell how a communist society should be organized or administered. His purpose, rather, was to explain what he called "the economic law of motion of modern society," that is, the factors which first propel the growth and spread of capitalism, then bring about its inevitable decay and doom.

Marx knew that several economists before his time had taught, first, that the exchange values or prices of goods depended solely upon the quantities of labor embodied in them and, second, that the wages paid to the workers who produced the goods would be barely enough to provide for their subsistence. Combining these two hypotheses, he concluded that the difference between the prices charged and the wages paid was a surplus value that rightfully belonged to the workers but was appropriated by their employers, who thereby became richer and richer.

Marx was greatly impressed by the growth of machine technology and large-scale production. As a result of this development, he argued, the larger firms would swallow the smaller firms, and wealth would become concentrated in fewer and fewer hands. At the same time, the workers would experience increasing misery. Society would be divided between a small group of big *capitalists* and an increasing mass of poverty-stricken workers or *proletarians*, whose ranks would be swollen by the dispossessed *petit-bourgeois* —former shopkeepers, small traders, and small industrialists forced out of business by the big capitalists. The class of big capitalists and the class of proletarians would engage in constant class warfare.

Business crises would occur periodically, largely because employers would not pay workers enough to enable them to consume the goods they had produced. Each crisis would be worse than the last, until finally capitalism would be destroyed. The proletariat would seize power and establish a new order. The class struggle would come to an end.

This, in a nutshell, was the Marxian prophecy. Little of what Marx argued and predicted is accepted today. The labor theory of value, and its twin theory of workers' exploitation designed to squeeze "surplus value" out of their work, were abandoned long ago by most economists. Labor is one, but not the only, creator of value; capital and entrepreneurship also contribute and are therefore entitled to part of what Marx called surplus value. In industrial countries, ownership did become more concentrated during the nineteenth century, but concentration has not noticeably increased during the twentieth. The condition of the working class, instead of getting worse, has greatly improved, both absolutely and relative to other classes. The middle class has grown proportionately larger. Class conflict has declined. Business depressions have largely been brought under control. The Communist revolution predicted by Marx has not occurred in the industrial countries, such as Great Britain, Germany, or the United States; instead it has come in a different form to preindustrial countries such as Russia and China.

This is not to say that Marxism is irrelevant in the modern world. The political doctrines of Marx, as interpreted and extended by V. I. Lenin and Mao Tse-tung, play a powerful role both in the Communist world and in the developing nations of Latin America, Africa, and Asia. As we shall see, however, the economic problems and procedures of all these countries can be reviewed without recourse to Marxist theory.


## THE WORLD'S ECONOMIES

**The tasks of economic organization**   Economic decisions must be made in any society, whatever its form of organization. What work shall each person engage in, for what reward? Which goods and services are to be produced, in what amounts and of what quality? Goods can be made in many different ways, using alternative combinations of labor, machinery, and other inputs; which production methods should be chosen? Since regions and their people differ in resources and special abilities, society must decide where, by whom, and on what scale each activity should be pursued and how the resulting output should be exchanged with other people and regions. How much of this year's production should go to current consumption, and how much should go into health and education (to improve "human capital") or new plant and equipment (physical capital), so that future consumption can be greater?

These are the problems of economic organization. The answer to each question influences answers to the other; they need to be coordinated for just and efficient economic performance. But how can "society" solve them and coordinate the decisions? Conceptually, there are two approaches. At one extreme there is the model of economic individualism; at the other, there is economic collectivism. We shall look at each in turn.

**Economic individualism**   In the model of economic individualism there is no central authority with power to make the essential decisions. Economic activity is guided, rather, by a multitude of individual decisions, each of them limited in scope. These decisions are then coordinated through the process of buying and selling at a price in free markets. In this model, consumers have sovereign power. When they enter the market to spend their incomes, what they do, in effect, is to cast dollar votes for the things they wish to have produced. Where they want more, they bid the price up; where they want less, the price falls. Individual entrepreneurs, exercising free initiative, seek to make a profit by producing and selling the things consumers want. To this end they enter the market to bid for the productive services of labor and capital. Entrepreneurs who produce the things consumers want more can pay more for resources; those who produce things wanted less can bid less. Workers, freely choosing their occupations, seek employment with the entrepreneurs who will pay the highest wage. Individuals, responding to the rate of interest, freely choose how much of their income they wish to save, entrusting their savings to the enterprises that promise the highest and safest returns.

Since profit is the motive that drives the entrepreneur, he might try to sell his product at a price far above his costs, or pay workers and stockholders amounts well below what others are paying. If he sets his price too high, he will prevent consumers from getting as much of his product as they would be willing to buy at a price that would cover its cost; if he offers to pay input-owners too little, he will not induce them to supply as much labor and capital for its production as consumers would wish to have employed. In fact, the entrepreneur is virtually prevented from following either course by the force of competition, because rival sellers will be willing to charge lower prices or pay higher wages and interest.

Prices therefore tend constantly to be equal to costs (where costs include an adequate profit for the owner). These prices then serve two simultaneous purposes: (1) Consumers are given an accurate basis for choosing among goods and services, and (2) workers and other input suppliers are offered alternative sources of income, accurately reflecting society's willingness to pay for their services. Their incomes in turn become the basis for consumer spending. Thus the circle is closed, and the short-run problems of economic organization are neatly solved.

The drive for profits also spurs alert individuals to apply modern science and technology in the search for new products and processes that will reduce costs and meet human needs more effectively. In this way the long-run direction and content of economic development will be guided by millions of individual judgments.

Economic individualism has distinctive political and ethical attributes. Control of the economy is completely democratic. Everyone who has a dollar can cast a vote. In an unrestricted market, there is no discrimination as to race, sex, or age. Voting goes on continuously, and producers respond, not only to the votes of the many who want one product, but also to the few who want another. It must be noted, however, that dollar voting is not on a one-person, one-vote basis. A rich person whose income is a hundred times as large as a poor person's will have a hundred times as many votes. This inequality is justified in principle on the ground that each person's income represents the value of his or her contribution to production.

The case for pure, unmodified economic individualism rests on five basic assumptions that may not be fulfilled. First, it is assumed that incomes will be obtained only by performing productive service. In practice, incomes may be obtained by inheriting wealth, by appropriating increases in the value of land, and by collecting monopoly profits, none of these being activities that render a service. Second, it is assumed that consumers are "sovereign" in that they are completely free to direct production toward the goods that will satisfy their tastes. In practice, their choices may be limited to those things that producers have chosen to produce, and their tastes may have been decisively shaped by advertising. Third, it is assumed that producers will be compelled by competitive forces to keep their prices close to their costs. In practice, producers may obtain and exert monopoly power that enables them to fix prices well above costs. Fourth, it is assumed that all costs, including those of environmental damage and pollution, will be counted by producers and covered in their selling price. In practice, such external costs may not be charged to producers and included in price, thus understating true costs and distorting the allocation of resources. Fifth, it is assumed that employers will compete freely in hiring workers and that workers will be well informed, mobile, and have access to higher wages and better jobs. In practice, labor markets may involve discrimination, or collusion on one or both sides, as well as inadequate knowledge of alternative opportunities. Because these five assumptions are not fully realized in practice, the pure model of economic individualism is modified in ways that we will be examining with some care.

**Economic collectivism**    Under economic individualism, productive enterprises are privately owned and managed. Under economic collectivism, ownership and management are in the hands of government. But this is not the most significant difference between the two. The difference is to be found, rather, in the contrasting methods employed in the two kinds of economy to determine the allocation of resources. Under individualism, allocation is determined by the process of buying and selling in free markets. Under collectivism it is determined by central decisions of the politico-economic managers of the entire system. The difference in method leads to a difference in results.

In a collectivist economy the allocation of resources is planned and controlled by a single authority. The process of decision-making is highly centralized, and each decision is broad in scope. Politically, the process is likely to involve a one-party regime. It could, however, be subject to democratic legislative influence.

If the society is governed by a mass party, economic sovereignty will lie with the party leadership. The "maximum leader(s)" will decide how much of the economy's effort is to be devoted to armament, how much to the creation of capital, how much to the needs of consumers. The resulting allocation of resources is not likely to be the one that consumers would freely choose. Ambitious national leaders will focus on building national power, ruthlessly tightening people's belts. An impatient modernizer will concentrate on defense-related heavy industry, ignoring agriculture and consumer welfare. Corrupt leaders will simply feather their nests.

If the society is governed by democratic political processes, ultimate sovereignty will lie with the voters. But the allocation of resources will be determined initially by the politicians and bureaucrats. Voters can influence the allocation to some extent by putting pressure on the legislature; they cannot control it in full detail. If they are dissatisfied, they can vote the government out of office. But they will be equally powerless to bring its successor under detailed control. The collectivist economy is less subject than the individualist economy to such control.

Prices do not fulfill the same function in the two economies.

Under economic individualism, prices reflect both the demand for goods and the costs incurred in producing them. In flexible markets, prices are the mechanism through which the free choices of consumers are compared with the free choices of those who control productive resources, so that the two groups of choices can be brought into equilibrium. Under economic collectivism, on the other hand, prices are employed as instruments to accomplish the purposes of the supreme authority. If the authority wishes to check the consumption of one commodity, it raises the price; if it wishes to encourage the consumption of another, it lowers the price. It need not charge each commodity with all the costs incurred in its production. It may sell one at a price that is well above its cost and another at a price that is well below cost, collecting extra receipts in the first case and paying a subsidy in the second. Individual decisions in a market economy respond to price signals; the collectivist economy manipulates prices almost at will.

Economic collectivism has marked practical advantages over the individualist economy. The collectivist economy, with its concentrated power, can move more readily to wage war. It can more easily direct resources into the investments its leaders think will spur development. It can organize large campaigns for sharp changes in the distribution of income or in traditional economic institutions. But these advantages are purchased at a price. The collectivist economy is less likely than the individualist economy to respect diversity among its citizens. And central decisions, although made on behalf of the people, are not in practice readily changed if they prove inefficient or harmful.

The case for economic collectivism rests upon five basic assuptions that may not be fulfilled. First, it is assumed that the central authority can collect, process, and evaluate promptly the information about people's wants that is needed to run a responsive economy. Second, it is assumed that the central authority can evaluate promptly and accurately an intricate body of data about alternative production costs. Third, it is assumed that the central authority can match up the data on people's wants and production costs and make economic decisions that will be acceptable to the members of that society. Fourth, it is assumed that the resulting rewards and penalities will elicit honest, efficient, productive work from everyone. Finally, it is assumed that the central authority, through wise foresight, can select proper economic development paths and induce people to follow them. Because these five assumptions are not easily realized in practice, the pure model of economic collectivism is modified in operation, as we shall see.

**Mixed economies**   Every economy in the world is a mixture containing elements of both individualism and collectivism. Along with the complications already noted, there are two further reasons for a mixed approach. First, the nature of some goods and services is such that they cannot be sold in separate units to certain individuals and withheld from their neighbors. How can "national defense" be supplied to some citizens but not to others? How can the services of a lighthouse be withheld from a passing ship that pays nothing? How can the cost of street lights be collected from all those who walk beneath them? Such "public goods," which account for a growing share of modern economic output, must be supplied by government, in amounts that are politically determined, and financed through taxation rather than customer purchase. Their production, however, may be most effectively carried on in the private sector.

A second reason relates to overall economic stability. An individualist market economy requires some governmental intervention, through fiscal and monetary management, to prevent the cycles of boom and bust that have plagued the past. Experience shows that Adam Smith's "invisible hand" leaves the system subject to drastic bouts of unemployment and inflation. Control of the money supply and aggregate spending is not provided for in an unregulated market economy.

Beyond this, governmental intervention is required in areas like municipal water supply and telephone service, where technology calls for a single supplier, or in areas like airlines and electric power, where the least-cost size of production unit is so large that a single producer or a very few producers can meet market demand. Competition is then bolstered by public regulation or replaced by public ownership. Governmental intervention is required also to limit the environmental damage that accompanies most production. Government-imposed effluent charges, for example, make firms pay for discharging wastes into their surroundings and encourage efforts to minimize these costs, at the same time making consumers aware of this part of the product's full production costs. Environmental quality standards and zoning ordinances are other examples of governmental instruments for regulating economic activity in the general interest.

Finally, the world's economies draw on both individualism and collectivism to guide and spur the process of economic development. Private entrepreneurs starting large development projects are sure to seek governmental support and protection, if not subsidies and guarantees. Central authorities in a collectivist economy, conversely, will seek to enlist energetic individual participation in the development programs launched by national planners. Coordination of large investments for mutual consistency and feasibility will be sought whatever the form of economic organization.

If they are all a mixture of individualism and collectivism, how can the world's economies be usefully classified? It is true that every economy displays both approaches. But the proportions of individualism and collectivism in the mix vary from country to country. In some countries individualism is dominant; in others, collectivism. Between the two, the difference in degree is so great that it becomes a difference in kind. In some economies the allocation of resources is very largely carried out through the market —these we shall designate *market economies*. In others, allocation is predominantly determined and directed by a central authority —these we shall designate *command economies*.

**The market economies**    The market economies, as we have defined them, include most of the countries of the world: the United States, the English-speaking countries of the British Commonwealth, the members of the European Community and most of the other countries in Western Europe, Japan, and most of the countries of Southeast Asia, the Middle East, Africa, and Latin America. In no other country except Canada has competition been maintained as it has in the United States. In nearly all these countries, public ownership has been carried further than in the United States; the railroads, airlines, telephone systems, and municipal utilities are usually in the hands of the government. Aside from this, public intervention in the economy is no more extensive in Canada or Australia, in Belgium, the Netherlands, West Germany, or Switzerland, in Japan, Mexico, or Brazil than it is in the United States. In many of the developing countries it is less extensive. In Great Britain, on the other hand, and in France and Italy, certain mining and manufacturing enterprises have been taken into public ownership. There, and in the Scandinavian countries, the government has intervened in the economy more extensively than in the United States. This is true, too, of such developing countries as India and Pakistan. Yet in all these countries the influence of the market is predominant.

**The command economies** The command economies clearly include the communist countries. In the Soviet Union and the Eastern European states of East Germany, Czechoslovakia, Poland, Hungary, Rumania, Albania, and Bulgaria, and in China, North Korea, Viet Nam, Cambodia, and Cuba, the economies conform more or less closely to the model of economic collectivism. Governments in most of these countries are now trying to make producers pay attention to consumers' tastes, but resource use is still publicly controlled. Yugoslavia, although it has much more private enterprise than its northern neighbors, must also be listed as a command economy. A few other countries appear to fall into this category. Spain has not been communistic in its ideology, but its economic system has been authoritarian. Egypt, Burma, and Indonesia have recently carried the nationalization of business enterprise to a point where the market has been superseded largely by public controls. Certain of the newly independent states of Africa seem to be moving in the same direction.

## THE PROCESS OF ECONOMIC DEVELOPMENT

The economies of the world today stand at different points in the process of development. A few still adhere to ancient methods of production and modes of life; these we may designate *traditional economies*. In many others, a modern sector has taken root and is spreading its influence to the traditional sector: these are the *developing economies*. In still others, modern science and technology have been applied throughout the economy, generating high levels of output and income; this group can be called *mature economies*. Finally, in at least one country, the outlines of a *post-industrial* stage of development are coming into view.

**Traditional economies** In a traditional society, men and women use hand tools, their children, and a few draft animals to scratch a bare living from an ill-understood environment. Fate seems to control their lives. Death rates are high and life expectancy is short. Birth rates must be high if each generation is to replace itself. Since a year's hard work by illiterate people in poor health produces very little output per person, most people are poor, especially where rulers and landlords extract a large share of output through taxes and rents from the peasantry. The nonagricultural parts of the economy are parasitic, absorbing rural output but contributing nothing to peasant life in the villages. The money value of annual output per person is around $100 or less.

Few countries remain in this category today, unaffected by the process of modernization. Parts of Central Africa qualify, along with Bhutan, Bangladesh, and Burma in south Asia, outlying parts of Indonesia and India, and of Haiti in the Caribbean.

**The content of development**  Economic development calls for new attitudes, attitudes fundamentally different from those that prevail in a traditional society. Some people, at least, have to be willing to try new ways of carrying on economic activity, take chances with new crops, put resources into new ventures. In the subsistence economy of a traditional society, each household produces mainly for itself, and each member has a known place. In a developed economy employing modern technology to produce high per capita incomes, individuals are tiny cogs in a vast, intricate web of mutual (and changing) interdependencies. The transition is painful, and it may take several generations of "economic development" for the necessary confident and adaptable attitudes to spread throughout the society.

Initially, development starts with a few people, in one or a few economic activities. Perhaps foreign entrepreneurs see an opportunity to start plantations on fertile land for an export crop, or mine a rich mineral deposit, or build an electric power plant in the capital city. Perhaps an alert minority within the traditional society responds to new opportunities by importing some looms for a small textile factory, or some buses for a bus line between the capital and the main port. There may be nationalistic political leaders who respond to pressures from foreign powers by subsidizing a rifle factory or small shipyard. For two centuries this process has spread across the world, differing only in detail from country to country and decade to decade.

Gradually, whatever the specific forms, modern science and

technology are applied in more and more activities, lowering costs, making people more productive, raising output per capita. There is a growing stock of physical capital (for example, developed land, mines, power plants, textile and other factories, bus lines, shipyards), all embodying contemporary technology. Mechanical and electrical power dramatically augment human and animal power in agriculture, transportation, and industry. The physical environment is reshaped to conform to human needs. The stock of "human capital" grows, too; people are healthier, more vigorous, longer-lived. Youth are kept out of the labor force to be educated, then placed in more productive careers than subsistence agriculture or silviculture. The whole population develops wider horizons, becomes more innovative and creative.

**Regional economic and political challenges**  Buying and selling activities put formerly isolated districts, regions, and continents in touch with each other. The positive benefits to all from specialization and exchange are very great, but so are the costs. The economic activities and regions that take the lead in development may pull far ahead of traditional activities and regions, undermining established political and social institutions and triggering violent reactions. National leaders have to find unifying solutions.

A poorly endowed country will need to import the raw materials it lacks. A country with diversified resources will still need to import modern technology, embodied in capital equipment and technical advisers. In both cases, exports will have to be generated to pay for the imports. Foreign aid or loans may give short-run support but in due course they must be repaid. The stern fact is, then, that economic development rests on promoting export activity in sectors and regions that can exchange profitably with the outside world. As modernization spreads to other sectors and regions, their per capita incomes will rise, eventually providing a domestic market for most of the economy's output.

**Developing economies**  Developing economies, whether old or young, are engaged in a long, difficult process that may run for a century or more as people learn to absorb unsettling changes in their ways of life. Migration from rural to urban areas uproots millions; familiar associations and standards give way to loneliness and anomie. Public health measures, such as malaria control and water purification, lower the death rate much more rapidly than the birth rate falls, so the population begins to grow rapidly. Because the infant death rate is cut sharply, the burden of dependency increases; the economy must feed, clothe, house, and educate thousands, even millions, who formerly would have died. In some developing countries today, over 40 percent of the population are under fifteen years of age. (In the United States, by contrast, the proportion is 28 percent.) Rates of unemployment and underemployment, especially in the crowded cities, are very high. National output rises, as modern methods raise productivity in more and more sectors of the economy, but individual incomes become more unequal as income-receivers in leading sectors pull away from the laggards. Tension and conflict may arise between the upwardly mobile groups in society and others who are being left behind.

Most economies in the world today can be categorized as developing. Some 80 countries fall into this group, with yearly per capita output varying from $130 to $3,000. They include China and India at the low end of the output range and Italy and Puerto Rico (a commonwealth within the United States) at the top.

**Mature economies**   In a mature economy, the application of modern science has spread to all economic activities. Agriculture employs only a minor share of the population; most people work in industry, transportation, construction, commerce and finance, government, education, or health care. Private consumption accounts for about 60 percent of total output, the other 40 percent going into capital formation and government services, financed by savings and taxes. The population, now predominantly urban, enjoys a low birth rate as well as a low death rate; population growth is modest, and a newborn child can expect to live 60 to 70 years. The people are literate, the labor force is mobile, markets are well organized, financial institutions are highly developed, and the central government is strong.

In this category one finds some 20 countries, mostly in Europe and North America, with total output per capita running from $3,220 in Czechoslovakia to $6,720 in Sweden and $6,650 in Switzerland. Some reached maturity early in this century, others only recently.

**The post-industrial economy**  The trends described above now seem to be leading to still a further stage of economic evolution, exemplified so far by the United States. The structure of output has shifted even more toward services; service occupations employ more than six-tenths of the labor force, while manufacturing industry's share is declining as agriculture's did earlier. Provision of health care, education, recreation, entertainment, and culture begins to rival the output of tangible commodities. Even in the production of final goods, raw materials account for a declining share of all the inputs, while intermediate processing services account for most of the total cost.

Where formerly the stress was on quantitative growth, attention shifts to qualitative considerations, and there is concern for the impact of growth on the quality of life. Bigger is no longer automatically better. Congestion throttles urban mobility. Air, water, and noise pollution foul the environment. Economists are forced to recognize that production of "goods" is accompanied by the production of "bads." The search for amenities brings disamenities in its wake.

There is growing recognition of the need to accommodate ourselves to our environment, use resources with care, anticipate the unwanted side effects that may accompany new products or processes. The United States' claims on energy and raw materials from the rest of the planet are already driving costs up; drastic economizing is a necessary response. What will this mean for ourselves and other countries?

**Comparative output per capita**  The contrasts among economies at the various stages of development can be crudely summed up in figures for their economic productivity. Table 1-1 shows the 1974 gross national product per person for 124 countries with a population of a million or more people. Countries are placed in five continental groups, with the highly productive economies heading each column and the poorest at the bottom. Comparing columns, one sees that European countries are mostly far above African countries; that GNP in the Middle East runs from $3,380 for Israel to $120 for Yemen; that in the Americas the range is between $6,640 for the United States and $140 for Haiti; and that in Asia, Australia's $4,760 is about 48 times as large as the figure for Bangladesh.

Although it is hard to measure accurately such widely differing

## TABLE 1-1

### Estimated Real Gross National Product Per Capita, by Continent and Country, 1974, in U.S. Dollars

| | THE AMERICAS | | EUROPE | | ASIA AND OCEANIA | | MIDDLE EAST AND NORTH AFRICA | | AFRICA, EXCEPT NORTH AFRICA | |
|---|---|---|---|---|---|---|---|---|---|---|
| **$3,000 OR OVER** | United States | 6,640 | Sweden | 6,720 | | | | | | |
| | Canada | 6,080 | Switzerland | 6,650 | | | | | | |
| | | | West Germany | 5,890 | | | | | | |
| | | | Denmark | 5,820 | | | | | | |
| | | | Norway | 5,280 | | | | | | |
| | | | Belgium | 5,210 | | | | | | |
| | | | France | 5,190 | | | | | | |
| | | | Netherlands | 4,880 | Australia | 4,760 | | | | |
| | | | Finland | 4,130 | New Zealand | 4,100 | | | | |
| | | | Austria | 4,050 | Japan | 3,880 | | | | |
| | | | East Germany | 3,430 | | | Israel | 3,380 | | |
| | | | United Kingdom | 3,360 | | | Libya | 3,360 | | |
| | | | Czechoslovakia | 3,220 | | | | | | |
| **$700 TO $2,990** | Puerto Rico | 2,400 | Italy | 2,770 | | | | | | |
| | Argentina | 1,900 | Poland | 2,450 | | | | | | |
| | Venezuela | 1,710 | Ireland | 2,370 | | | | | | |
| | Trinidad and Tobago | 1,490 | USSR | 2,300 | | | | | | |
| | Jamaica | 1,140 | Hungary | 2,140 | Singapore | 2,120 | Saudi Arabia | 2,080 | | |
| | Uruguay | 1,060 | Greece | 1,970 | | | Lebanon | 1,080 | | |
| | Panama | 1,010 | Spain | 1,960 | | | Iran | 1,060 | | |
| | Mexico | 1,000 | Bulgaria | 1,770 | | | Iraq | 970 | | |
| | Brazil | 900 | Portugal | 1,540 | Hong Kong | 1,540 | | | | |
| | Chile | 820 | Yugoslavia | 1,250 | | | | | South Africa | 1,200 |
| | Costa Rica | 790 | | | | | | | | |
| | Peru | 710 | | | Taiwan | 720 | | | | |
| **$400 TO** | Nicaragua | 650 | Turkey | 690 | Malaysia | 660 | Algeria | 650 | | |
| | Cuba | 640 | | | Mongolia | 620 | | | | |
| | Dominican Republic | 590 | | | | | | | | |
| | Guatamala | 570 | Albania | 530 | | | Tunisia | 550 | Angola | 580 |

**$690**

| Latin America | | Asia | | Middle East | | Africa | |
|---|---|---|---|---|---|---|---|
| Colombia | 510 | South Korea | 470 | Syria | 490 | Rhodesia | 480 |
| Paraguay | 480 | Papua, New Guinea | 440 | Morocco | 430 | Zambia | 480 |
| Guyana | 470 | | | Jordan | 400 | Mozambique | 420 |
| Ecuador | 460 | | | | | Ivory Coast | 420 |

**$130 TO $390**

| Latin America | | Asia | | Middle East | | Africa | |
|---|---|---|---|---|---|---|---|
| El Salvador | 390 | North Korea | 390 | Egypt | 280 | Congo | 380 |
| Honduras | 340 | Philippines | 310 | | | Ghana | 350 |
| Bolivia | 250 | China | 300 | | | Liberia | 330 |
| Haiti | 140 | Thailand | 300 | | | Senegal | 320 |
| | | South Vietnam | 170 | | | Cameroon | 260 |
| | | Indonesia | 150 | | | Nigeria | 240 |
| | | India | 130 | | | Mauritania | 230 |
| | | Pakistan | 130 | | | Togo | 210 |
| | | North Vietnam | 130 | | | Central African Rep. | 200 |
| | | Sri Lanka | 130 | | | Kenya | 200 |
| | | | | | | Sierra Leone | 180 |
| | | | | | | Malagasy Republic | 170 |
| | | | | | | Uganda | 160 |
| | | | | | | Zaire | 150 |
| | | | | | | Sudan | 150 |
| | | | | | | Tanzania | 140 |
| | | | | | | Malawi | 130 |

**LESS THAN $130**

| Asia | | Middle East | | Africa | |
|---|---|---|---|---|---|
| Nepal | 110 | Yemen, Arab Rep. | 120 | Guinea | 120 |
| Bangladesh | 100 | Yemen, P.D. Rep. | 120 | Dahomey | 120 |
| Afghanistan | 100 | | | Lesotho | 120 |
| Burma | 90 | | | Niger | 100 |
| Bhutan | 70 | | | Ethiopia | 90 |
| | | | | Chad | 90 |
| | | | | Upper Volta | 80 |
| | | | | Rwanda | 80 |
| | | | | Burundi | 80 |
| | | | | Somalia | 80 |
| | | | | Mali | 70 |

SOURCE: Rearranged from IBRD, *World Bank Atlas* (Washington, 1976).

levels of output, these figures properly portray the extreme contrasts that now exist across the world. This does not mean that the average U.S. citizen is exactly 95 times as well off ($6,640 divided by $70) as the typical Malian. For one thing, the World Bank's estimates presented in Table 1-1 are based on currency exchange rates that take no account of the value of the nonmarketed output of subsistence farmers. And since personal consumption is a smaller fraction of total output in high-output countries than in those at the bottom, the contrasts in household consumption are smaller than those in per capita product. But a thirtyfold difference from Central Africa to North America is not implausible, and the human implications are profound. Are these differences permanent? Can the poor countries ever catch up?

## RATES OF ECONOMIC GROWTH

The search for answers leads to a review of recent growth experience. Because gains in economic welfare require that an economy's output grow more rapidly than its population, we look at the rates of output growth and population growth that rich and poor countries have recently been experiencing and note some of the forces at work. Some countries in the middle are starting to catch up, but the poorest are lagging behind in growth of output per capita. Moreover, the development process increases income inequality within a society during the period of catching up, until a high level of per capita income is reached. We note, finally, that there are limits to growth.

**Recent experience in output growth**  Table 1-2 shows that from 1960 through 1973, the 25 countries with the largest gross national products all experienced substantial growth of output. In most countries, output grew between 4 and 6 percent per year. The star was Japan, where output grew almost 11 percent annually. Iranian output grew almost 10 percent annually, while in the United Kingdom the rate was under 3 percent. These averages shift somewhat if different periods are considered, and the estimates are not very precise. It is clear nonetheless that, in most large economies, output has been expanding until recently, and that (since anything growing at 5 percent annually will double in size in 14 years) these growth rates are impressive.

## TABLE 1-2
## Growth Rates of Total Product, 1960–73, in the 25 Countries with the Largest 1974 Gross National Products

| COUNTRY | 1974 GNP (billions of dollars) | 1960–73 AVERAGE ANNUAL OUTPUT GROWTH RATE (percent) |
|---|---|---|
| United States | 1,407 | 4.3 |
| USSR | 581 | 5.3[a] |
| Japan | 426 | 10.6 |
| West Germany | 365 | 4.6 |
| France | 272 | 5.7 |
| China | 246 | 5.6[b] |
| United Kingdom | 189 | 2.9 |
| Italy | 153 | 5.0 |
| Canada | 137 | 5.4 |
| Brazil | 93 | 6.6 |
| Poland | 82 | 4.8 |
| India | 79 | 3.5[c] |
| Spain | 69 | 7.0 |
| Netherlands | 66 | 5.3 |
| Australia | 63 | 5.1 |
| East Germany | 59 | 3.0 |
| Mexico | 58 | 6.9 |
| Sweden | 55 | 3.7 |
| Belgium | 51 | 4.8 |
| Czechoslovakia | 47 | 2.9 |
| Argentina | 47 | 4.2 |
| Switzerland | 43 | 4.3 |
| Iran | 35 | 9.8 |
| Austria | 30 | 4.9 |
| Denmark | 29 | 4.6 |

[a] See Chapter 5, p. 125.
[b] See Chapter 2, p. 50.
[c] See Chapter 3, p. 71.

SOURCE: Derived from data in IBRD, *World Bank Atlas*, 1975, except as noted.

The countries listed in Table 1-2 are at various stages along the road to development—India and China emerging from the traditional-society phase, and the United Kingdom and United States turning a new corner, with many individual variations between these extremes. Our subsequent chapters are case studies of several of these economies, designed to illuminate the variety of forces at work. Here we suggest only a rather disturbing implication of the growth rates shown in Table 1-2.

Advanced countries continue to grow, quite rapidly, and thus are hard to catch up with. Growth is easier for a mature economy than for a developing economy for three basic reasons. First, the mature economy has an ample surplus over and above its private household consumption, a surplus that is regularly plowed back into growth-promoting outlays on capital, both physical and human, by individuals and by governments. In the early stages of development the margin above subsistence is too slender to permit the investments needed for rapid growth. Thus, in the Appalachian phrase, "Them as has, gits." Second, the mature economy has an intricate network of institutions for organizing and coordinating economic expansion, while the developing economy is not yet so equipped. Third, the people of a mature economy are more used to change, more adaptive, and more forward-looking than those emerging from a traditional society. Growth is neither painless nor automatic anywhere, but it is easier for the rich than for the poor.

**Recent experience in population growth**   In Table 1-3 we rank the 25 countries with the largest populations, divided into those with high per capita GNPs and those with medium or low per capita GNPs in 1974. For each, we show the average annual rate of growth of its population between 1960 and 1973. The high-income countries had modest rates of population growth, between 0.5 and 1.2 percent per year. In low-income countries, populations grew at 2.0 to 3.5 percent per year. The contrast, seemingly minor, is in fact disastrous. At 3.5 percent, a population doubles in 20 years. If annual population growth is 1.0 percent, a country will have not 20, but 70, years in which to accommodate the doubling of its total population. In developed countries where output growth is relatively easy, population growth has been modest, while the countries facing major difficulties in ex-

## TABLE 1-3
### Population Growth Rates, 1960–73, in the 25 Countries with the Largest 1974 Populations

| HIGH GNP-PER-CAPITA COUNTRIES | | | MEDIUM OR LOW GNP-PER-CAPITA COUNTRIES | | |
|---|---|---|---|---|---|
| COUNTRY | 1974 POPULATION (millions) | AVERAGE ANNUAL GROWTH RATE (percent) | COUNTRY[a] | 1972 POPULATION (millions) | AVERAGE ANNUAL GROWTH RATE (percent) |
| USSR | 252 | 1.1 | China[a] | 920 | 2.1 |
| United States | 212 | 1.2 | India | 596 | 2.3 |
| Japan | 109 | 1.1 | Indonesia | 127 | 2.0 |
| West Germany | 62 | 0.9 | Brazil | 104 | 2.9 |
| United Kingdom | 56 | 0.5 | Bangladesh | 76 | 2.6 |
| Italy | 55 | 0.7 | Nigeria | 73 | 2.5 |
| France | 53 | 1.0 | Pakistan | 68 | 2.9 |
| Spain | 35 | 1.1 | Mexico | 58 | 3.5 |
| Poland | 34 | 0.9 | Philippines | 41 | 3.0 |
| | | | Thailand | 41 | 3.1 |
| | | | Turkey | 39 | 2.5 |
| | | | Egypt | 36 | 2.5 |
| | | | South Korea | 33 | 2.2 |
| | | | Iran | 33 | 3.2 |
| | | | Burma | 30 | 2.2 |
| | | | Ethiopia | 27 | 2.2 |

[a] See Chapter 2, pp. 50 and 53.

SOURCE: Rearranged from IBRD, *World Bank Atlas,* 1975, except as noted.

*Merging traffic*

panding their output are precisely the ones burdened with rapid population growth.

A population grows when birth rates exceed death rates. Countries with high birth rates are countries whose death rates have been very high, making high birth rates necessary for the population's survival. One central human feature of the modernization process is a "demographic transition" from the high death and birth rates of traditional peasant life to the low death and birth rates of modern urban life. In Europe the transition took almost a century, during which populations expanded markedly, since death rates fell before birth rates did. Now this transition has begun in Asia, Africa, and Latin America, but in a form much harder to manage. Preventive health measures such as malaria control are now relatively easy to apply, so death rates have fallen dramatically since 1945, far more rapidly than they did in nineteenth-century Europe and America. Since age of marriage and size of family are personal decisions not easily changed by distant authorities, the excess of births over deaths has led to the population growth rates shown in Table 1-3.

**Recent experience in per capita growth rates**  When expanding output must be divided among a larger population, output per capita grows less rapidly than absolute output. If output rises 50 percent in a decade while population grows by 20 percent, per capita output goes up by 25 percent ($150/120 = 1.25$).

Table 1-4 shows 1960–1973 rates of per capita output growth for the 25 countries with the highest rates over this period. One sees that many smaller countries have raised per capita output rapidly. Three oil-exporting countries appear high in the list, and, of course, when more recent years are counted their number will increase. Five vigorous Asian economies, led by Japan, have raised output per capita at impressive rates. The only large economies among the first 25 here are Japan and France. Israel, whose population growth rate (including immigration) was 3.1 percent, raised its GNP at an average annual rate of 8.9 percent, thus yielding a per capita gain of 5.6 percent per year. There is great diversity in size, income level, stage of development, and form of economic organization among the countries listed; neither market economies nor command economies as a group displayed clear superiority in growth performance. Among the low-growth countries (not shown in Table 1-4), one finds, however, the largest and poorest (China, India, Indonesia, Bangladesh, Nigeria) accounting for over 1.8 billion people, with the growth rate of per capita output varying from 3.4 percent in China down to zero growth in Bangladesh.

**Income inequality during the development process**  Economic development enables countries to raise their output more

## TABLE 1-4
### Per Capita GNP Growth, 1960–73, in the 25 Countries with the Fastest Growth Rates in GNP Per Capita

| COUNTRY | GNP PER CAPITA (1973 DOLLARS) | | 13-YEAR GAIN | AVERAGE ANNUAL GROWTH RATE (percent) |
|---|---|---|---|---|
| | 1960 | 1973 | | |
| Libya | 960 | 3,530 | 2,570 | 10.5 |
| Japan | 1,130 | 3,630 | 2,500 | 9.4 |
| Saudi Arabia | 540 | 1,610 | 1,070 | 8.7 |
| Portugal | 560 | 1,410 | 850 | 7.4 |
| Greece | 750 | 1,870 | 1,120 | 7.3 |
| South Korea | 160 | 400 | 240 | 7.1 |
| Singapore | 750 | 1,830 | 1,080 | 7.1 |
| Hong Kong | 590 | 1,430 | 840 | 7.0 |
| Taiwan | 280 | 660 | 380 | 6.9 |
| Iran | 390 | 870 | 480 | 6.4 |
| Spain | 820 | 1,710 | 890 | 5.8 |
| Puerto Rico | 1,060 | 2,180 | 1,120 | 5.7 |
| Israel | 1,480 | 3,010 | 1,530 | 5.6 |
| Yugoslavia | 560 | 1,060 | 500 | 5.1 |
| Thailand | 150 | 270 | 120 | 4.8 |
| France | 2,500 | 4,540 | 2,040 | 4.7 |
| Bulgaria | 880 | 1,590 | 710 | 4.7 |
| North Korea | 190 | 340 | 150 | 4.6 |
| Papua, New Guinea | 230 | 410 | 180 | 4.6 |
| Finland | 2,030 | 3,600 | 1,570 | 4.5 |
| Austria | 2,010 | 3,510 | 1,500 | 4.4 |
| Albania | 260 | 460 | 200 | 4.4 |
| Togo | 220 | 380 | 160 | 4.4 |
| Panama | 530 | 920 | 390 | 4.4 |
| Italy | 1,420 | 2,450 | 1,030 | 4.3 |

SOURCE: Derived from estimates in IBRD, *World Bank Atlas*, 1975.

rapidly than their population, but all members of society do not benefit equally from the gains. Experience in dozens of countries shows, in fact, that people in the lower 60 percent of the income distribution are likely not only to fall behind those who spurt ahead, but even to suffer an absolute fall in their real incomes during the early and middle stages of reorganizing a traditional society.[1] Handicraft occupations may be displaced and landless peasants may be pushed out of agriculture, while at the same time population starts growing rapidly and living costs may rise markedly. Only a small minority of the population benefits directly from the modern activities getting under way in a few regions of the country, and there may be "backwash effects" on other people and regions that last for a couple of generations. With time, the benefits of development spread to the middle segment of the population and eventually the incomes of the poor begin to rise. Much depends on where political power lies, what resources the country has, and what deliberate policies are pursued. Typically, in the late stages of modernization, extreme income inequalities are reduced and the broad gains of modernization are widely shared. But there is ample room for improvement over the past in the way the intervening changes are managed in the countries traversing this road.

**Interacting pressures of growth**    Over the last quarter century, as we have seen, economic growth has accelerated over most of the world. One unfortunate result has been increasing pressure on world resources and a growing tendency toward chronic inflation. Many factors are involved. In developed economies the unrelenting pursuit of domestic full employment has kept demand high, stimulated raw material imports, and encouraged resource-using technology. Prosperity in many middle-income countries has resulted in dietary changes, raising demand in world markets for various items, such as feedgrains for livestock. The grain and sugar reserves that provided a cushion against bad harvests during the 1950s and 1960s are no longer available. The advantages of oil and gas over coal led most of the world to switch fuels, whereupon the OPEC (Organization of Petroleum Exporting Countries) nations found that royalties (scarcity rents) on their ample

[1] See Irma Adelman and Cynthia Taft Morris, *Economic Growth and Social Equity in Developing Countries* (Stanford: Stanford University Press, 1973), pp. 178–83.

supplies could be much higher than the international oil companies had disclosed to them.

As everyone knows, higher prices have been the result. Flexible market economies are responding through a series of substitutions (small cars for large, apartments for houses-on-an-acre-each, cellulose for petrochemicals) that will lessen the blow to living standards. The tragic victims have been the peasants of Bangladesh, India, Pakistan, and other countries without primary products they can sell at a premium in world markets. When fuel and petroleum-based fertilizers quadruple in price, marginal farmers are squeezed out. The OPEC authorities have so far done little for them, and developed nations have not yet worked out ways to organize a practical new structure of relationships.

Until recently, a misadventure in one economy had only limited ill effect upon other economies; a failed harvest in India or Brazil or Ghana might plunge that country into recession or inflation or both, but the event could safely be ignored by most or all other countries. That is much less true than formerly. With few exceptions the world's economies are intertwined. Those that do not trade with one another for vital goods and services compete with one another in the purchase and sale of foodstuffs, fuels, raw materials, and manufactures in world markets. In parody of poet John Donne, "No economy is an island unto itself / therefore never send to know for whom the costs and prices rise / They rise for thee."

**The limits to growth**  When considering the prospects for continued growth by the world's economies, we must take care to avoid the fallacy of composition—that is, the naive thought that what has been true for one economy or a few can also be true for *all* economies taken as a group. Contrary to general belief only a few years ago, there are limits to the world's, as opposed to one economy's, industrial growth. What are these limits, and how rapidly are they being approached?

The main fact to confront is that our planet contains a finite rather than unlimited amount of the physical ingredients with which goods and (to a lesser extent) services are produced and consumed: arable land, fresh water, minerals, forests, and oceans. Many of the most important, like coal and oil, are strictly non-renewable. And although others, like farm land, are renewable, their renewal is usually dependent upon their extensive treatment with exhaustible resources such as chemical fertilizers. The more rapid the rate of utilization of these ingredients, the sooner will their supply be depleted and the growth process brought to a halt.

At present growth rates, the evil day can be postponed in only two ways, both of which are themselves costly in real terms. One is to enlarge the pool of resources by discoveries on Earth or elsewhere in the universe. Whether the resources gained by discovery will exceed those consumed in the effort is a question that only time and experience can answer. The other way is through technological innovation (for example, electric power output per pound of coal burned has risen severalfold during the last half-century) or through substitution of relatively plentiful resources for relatively scarce ones (for example, the replacement of steel products with plastics in many applications). But technological change has limits too: it is costly, time-consuming, often has very unattractive side effects, and—most important of all—can only delay the inevitable.

Even if resources were unlimited, exponential growth in the world's output into the indefinite would be most unlikely. Growth generates external diseconomies in the form of environmental degradation that poisons growth: spoliation of the land and pollution of the air, water, and climate. Certain of these diseconomies are avoidable or reparable; forests can be regrown, grasslands restored, waste emissions recycled. But

> There remains one barrier that confronts us with all the force of an ultimatum from nature. It is that industrial production, including, of course, the extraction of resources, requires the use of energy, and that all energy, including that generated from natural processes such as wind power or solar radiation, is inextricably involved with the emission of heat.[2]

Currently, man is adding only negligibly to the atmospheric heat naturally generated by the sun and the earth itself. But if industrial output continues to expand in mature economies and massive industrial growth takes hold in poor countries as well, energy use will multiply rapidly and within a century or so world temperatures will rise prohibitively. Technological progress, substitutions, and other adjustments will surely avert imminent disaster,

[2] Robert Heilbroner, *An Inquiry into the Human Prospect* (New York: W. W. Norton, 1974), p. 50.

but as Robert Heilbroner suggests, "even under the most optimistic or unrealistic assumptions with regard to resource availability or technology, [there may well be an] inescapable need to limit industrial growth."[3]

The message for mankind is clear and unequivocal. All the world's economies must learn to produce goods without concurrently degrading the environment and, more importantly, at the same time sharply curtail production of goods having a substantial natural-resources content. Even under these conditions, real income the world over can continue to rise, provided that the time and labor now devoted to industrial output are reallocated to activities that in all respects make life better yet require relatively small amounts of resources and generate relatively little heat.

## STANDARDS OF ECONOMIC PERFORMANCE

The standards we use in judging the performance of any economy depend upon our values. If we value physical comfort, we ask that the economy produce plenty. If we value freedom, we ask that it permit individual choice. If we value justice, we ask that the economy provide equality of opportunity. If we value stability, we ask that it run smoothly. If our population is increasing and our wants are rising, we ask that the economy grow.

The weight given to each standard varies from society to society. Moreover, the goals may conflict with each other. It may be necessary to choose between equity and plenty, between plenty and stability, between stability and freedom, between freedom and growth. The choices made will reflect each society's ruling values.

However the society ranks its values, and whatever the weights each reader has in mind, we find it useful in this book to judge each economy according to these standards: plenty, freedom, equity, stability, and growth. Let us examine them.

**Plenty**  First of all, people everywhere have basic needs for food, shelter, and clothing. Beyond this, modern knowledge and efficient economic organization can respond to a vast range of further desires. People want medical care, good health, and long life. People

[3] *Ibid.*, p. 54.

want tools and machines to relieve toil and raise their productive power. They want an education for their children, to improve their opportunities and widen their horizons. These needs and desires are especially vital at low levels of per capita income. The rich, of course, have further desires: second homes, world tours, pleasure boats, snowmobiles. If people are to have these things, their economy must become developed and must use its resources efficiently. The first question to ask, therefore, in judging the performance of an economy, is whether it produces plenty.

**Economic freedom**  Economic freedom comes from having choices. As societies modernize, men and women increasingly look for access to a variety of occupations, rather than having their work assigned to them. They want to be able to defy authority without having all their job opportunities closed off. They want to move elsewhere or stay put, as they choose, without government coercion or restriction. People value the right to make their own choices among consumer goods, instead of having goods selected for them. They want liberty to choose: among occupations, among places, among goods. The second question to ask of an economy, then, is whether it permits freedom of choice.

**Economic justice**  The desire for economic justice grows with modernization. As income grows and wealth increases, issues of equitable sharing gain weight. Most people do not ask for complete equality of income or wealth; they do ask an equal chance to acquire them. They want an economy where doors are not closed on the basis of race, sex, age, or religion. They want an economy where neither party to a bargain can take undue advantage of the other. They want an economy where rewards are related to effort and skill, not privilege and monopoly. In an equitable economy, the existing differences in income and wealth are seen by its members as just and necessary. The third question to ask of an economy is whether it provides economic justice.

**Economic stability and security**  The importance of economic stability arises out of the threat of prolonged unemployment and chronic inflation. As people become bound up in a network of interdependence, they want insurance against a malfunctioning system. They want an economy that provides reasonable steadiness in job opportunities and in the cost of living. They want an economy that makes provisions against individual economic disasters: disabling accidents, major diseases, helpless old age. In a stable, well-functioning economy, a lifetime of individual participation will ensure a decent old age. The fourth question to ask of an economy, therefore, is whether it runs smoothly.

**Growth**   In a world where most people are poor, and where low-income populations are growing rapidly, output growth is urgently desired. Men and women want more for themselves and their children. They want jobs, housing, schools and hospitals, tools to work with and factories to work in. All these require increased output. In a developed economy with high per capita incomes, output growth is still needed as long as the population is growing. Added output will also accompany efforts to reduce environmental contamination, since the efforts themselves add to the flow of useful activity. And as cost-reducing or quality-enhancing innovations displace old products and processes, genuine economic welfare increases and measured output grows. Thus, in spite of income-inequality problems that arise in the course of economic development, and in spite of ultimate limits to growth, the final question to ask of an economy is whether it is growing.

## THE ECONOMIES WE STUDY

The economies of the world are numerous and diverse. Many of them would repay detailed study. Brazil, the key country in South America, would stand as an example of a large neighbor experiencing rapid growth through a mixture of private enterprise and military government. Yugoslavia would reveal a developing collectivist economy practicing "market socialism" strikingly different from the procedures found in the USSR and China. Japan would present the only instance so far of an old Asian society to have attained economic maturity. Analysis of Argentina would reveal an economy that, although well endowed, has so far failed to achieve sustained growth.

Our space, however, is limited; accordingly, our sample must be small. We start with China, the most populous country in the world and the one whose massive efforts to break out of a traditional society present the greatest contrast with Western experience. We move on to India, an equally ancient Asian society that has tried through democratic means to grow out of a very difficult position. In Chapter 4 we turn to Mexico, our southern neighbor, now achieving rapid growth through a mixture of institutions—market, communal, and governmental. We then examine the Soviet economy—large, powerful, and lopsided, currently struggling to adapt the institutions of a command economy to the needs of a developed society. Turning West, in Chapter 6 we consider the European Community, a group of nine countries that have modernized separately but are now seeking further gains through the elimination of all barriers to exchange of inputs and outputs among themselves. With the perspective thus gained, in Chapter 7 we evaluate the record of the United States' economy, which has grown to mature affluence under fortunate circumstances and is now the first economy to confront the problems of "post-industrial society."

## SUGGESTED READINGS

Black, E. C., *The Dynamics of Modernization: A Study in Comparative History*. Harper Torchbooks TB 1321. New York: Harper & Row, 1966.

A compact interdisciplinary review by an eminent historian.

Kuznets, Simon, *Modern Economic Growth: Rate, Structure and Spread*. New Haven, Conn.: Yale University Press, 1966.

———, *Economic Growth of Nations: Total Output and Production Structure*. Cambridge, Mass.: Harvard University Press, 1971.

Detailed quantitative analysis by a great economic historian.

Lewis, W. Arthur, *Development Economics: An Outline*. Module 20 30V 00. Morristown, New Jersey: General Learning Press, 1974.

A wise, compressed, demanding summary by an experienced economist.

Meadows, Donella H., *et al.*, *The Limits to Growth* (1972), together with Cole, H. S. D., *et al.*, editors. *Models of Doom: A Critique of the Limits to Growth* (1973), both published by Universe Books, 381 Park Avenue South, New York, N.Y.

*Limits* is a popular, unsubstantiated statement of the problem; *Models* presents a dozen critical comments and a rebuttal by the Meadows group.

# CHINA 2

We begin with China, a very large country whose economy provides the sharpest kind of contrast with our own. China was old, rich, and powerful before the United States was born. The last two centuries have seen the United States grow to unprecedented wealth and power. The same period saw a gradual collapse of traditional Chinese society. Now the ancient structure has been fully overturned and a new organization of society has taken shape. The Chinese people are poor, four times as numerous as Americans, and tightly organized in a collective drive for modernization.

During their 26 years in power, the Chinese Communists have launched the most rapid and far-reaching transformation of society ever attempted. The new regime has brought under firm control the full territory of the Middle Kingdom—China's name for itself as the center of its world for over two thousand years. Agricultural output has kept pace with population growth. Industrial production has grown very rapidly. Most fundamentally, the major institutions and traditions of Chinese civilization have been undermined and new institutions and attitudes have been put in their place. While Soviet advisers and equipment helped in the first decade, the new regime has experimentally developed its own distinctively Chinese way of modernizing.

The following section of this chapter describes the forms of Chinese economic organization that currently shape the country's life. We go on to review China's development experience since 1949. Then we analyze China's record of growth in output and population. The chapter ends with an evaluation of Chinese performance in terms of the standards laid down in Chapter 1.

# CURRENT CHINESE ECONOMIC ORGANIZATION

The course of China's command economy is set in accordance with the state's purposes, yet it operates in flexible and decentralized fashion. Individual efforts are carefully linked to public goals. Decisions are collective rather than individual, yet self-reliance is promoted and rewards reflect individual effort.

**Control organs at four levels**   China is a one-party state in which a large and highly active Communist Party stands behind and above the regular government. The usual government offices exist, together with a large network of state-owned mines, mills, factories, trading firms, and other economic agencies. The armed forces are large, and army units have a significant role in economic activity. The sharing of power among party, government, and army organs has on occasion generated friction and uncertainty.

Management of the huge Chinese economy is organized at four geographic and administrative levels. National authority is concentrated at Peking. Below this lie 26 provinces with populations ranging from 2 million to 98 million people each, with an average of 35 million, or more than the entire population of most of the world's nation states. Provinces contain numerous counties, each a distinct economic entity. At the bottom lie some 50,000 communes, basic units of local administration. The commune is a new economic organization, but county, provincial, and national bodies reflect many centuries of Chinese practice.

**The Chinese commune today**   Throughout rural China, and in cities as well, local economic administration is guided by the commune. A commune contains from 1,000 to 5,000 families engaged in farming and other activities. It is divided into several brigades of 100 to 200 households, and brigades in turn are subdivided into teams that correspond roughly to small villages. The work of each team is managed by its members, under now well-established guidelines, and the incomes of members depend on their work. The village is drawn into larger projects at the brigade level, and on occasion the whole commune will be involved in a large-scale effort. Pressure from central authorities reaches every household, yet the complex hierarchy allows for local initiative and a good deal of diversity. Observers familiar with economic life in other developing countries, or with earlier periods in Chinese history, are impressed with the effective, honest, tough-minded rural administration they see in contemporary China.

**Consumption management**   A basic feature of Chinese life today is an assured minimum of food, shelter, and clothing for everyone. Standard monthly rations of foodgrain and cooking oil provide a basic diet. An annual ration of cloth is enough for a simple wardrobe, and housing assignments are designed to assure separate though crowded quarters for every family. These staples are available at prices that have remained unchanged for many years. A state trading network sells the basic food and clothing rations everywhere, having acquired them previously from state factories, communes, and peasants at controlled prices.

In addition to this foundation of rationed supplies, a wide variety of other foods and consumer goods is available through the market. Fresh vegetables and fruit, meat, fish, and poultry, even wines and spirits, are available at prices that vary seasonally and regionally but remain within the reach of most households. These extras are produced by communes located near urban markets and by peasants on their private plots. A substantial part of farm income is earned this way. Clothing beyond the basic ration, sewing machines, bicycles, and a great variety of consumer goods are available through the state trading network.

The level of farm and nonfarm incomes in China now suffices to cover the simple consumer market basket sketched above. Elementary education for children and medical care for all are also available; education is provided without charge, and medical care is supplied at nominal cost. Beyond these goods and services, however, moral incentives rather than material incentives are relied on to elicit effort and reward performance. Wide disparities of income and consumption are not permitted. The issue is vital, and we shall return to it later.

**Production management**   Chinese national economic planning at present is confined to a handful of major industrial outputs such as electric power and steel, along with basic agricultural products such as wheat, rice, and cotton. National targets are set each year in physical terms, and more detailed implications are worked out at provincial, city, and county levels. Information on procedures is sketchy and the plans themselves have not been published for 15 years, but the still-simple requirements of the

Chinese economy at this stage do appear to be adequately co-ordinated.

In designing consumer goods, for example, Chinese factories evidently rely on the judgment of the sales organization that distributes their products so that unsold goods do not accumulate. Plans for expanding output seem to be set at reachable levels. In both respects, current Chinese production planning appears more sensible, as we shall see, than Soviet planning.

The most striking aspect of current Chinese production management is the way all available men and women are brought into production, in the countryside as well as in the cities. As we saw in Chapter 1, developing economies typically have trouble finding productive work for peasants in the off season and for all those who are displaced by modern industry. In Chinese rural areas, abundant labor is drawn on in four ways: (1) Small-scale industry has been deliberately launched wherever possible, (2) road building and other construction projects have taken up the slack in idle seasons, (3) more extensive irrigation has permitted the planting of two or more crops per year over a wider area, and (4) diversification of agriculture into various specialities has drawn on labor not involved in grain growing. This point is further developed in what follows.

**Regional self-sufficiency and coordination**  Instead of trying to manage China as a single, tightly organized economy, the regime now calls for regional self-sufficiency and local self-reliance. Twenty-five years ago, Chinese industry was concentrated in Shanghai, Hankow, a few other port cities, and Manchuria. Major efforts have since been made to build new industrial centers away from the coast and to spread small-scale industry very widely throughout the country. One motive has been protection against invasion from the north. Another motive has been a desire to strengthen each region's ability to solve its problems without depending on the center. This kind of decentralized management has been facilitated, of course, by the four-tiered pyramid of administrative bodies. And firms could be successfully transferred to local authorities because they "generally purchased most of their intermediate inputs from organizations located within the same province (or cities) and sold their output there as well."[1]

[1] See Dwight H. Perkins, "Plans and Their Implementation in the PRC," *American Economic Review* (May 1973), pp. 227–28.

Small-scale firms are centered mainly in five lines of production: iron and steel products, cement, chemical fertilizer, energy (coal and electricity), and the production and repair of farm tools and machinery. Their output supplies nearby agricultural customers or contributes to nearby capital construction projects. Production costs may be relatively high in these small factories but there may be offsetting gains in promptness of delivery, flexibility of output, and reduced transportation costs.

The drive to develop small-scale industry in rural areas is linked with a system of strong controls designed to hold back the massive migration from rural to urban areas that has been a major feature of the modernization process all over the world. Chinese social controls suppress this movement in three ways: (1) One cannot legally get a job except through a city's central employment bureau, (2) occupancy of living quarters is conditional upon having a registered job, and (3) permission to change one's residence is required from the authorities who ration food and clothing. Not only are rural people prevented from migrating freely to the city, but urban boys and girls, after nine years of school (sometimes twelve), are required to go out to rural areas for at least two years before having a chance to compete for an urban career.

Chinese efforts to promote regional self-sufficiency are aided by the long-established structure of the major provinces of the country. Most provinces are densely populated and large enough to take the full output of local plants with reasonable economies of scale. Agriculture in these densely settled provinces, especially where local transport costs are high because of mountainous terrain or poor roads, feeds into a network of trading channels through which products generally move only short distances from producer to user. The activities of small-scale industry can readily build upon and extend these local channels but need not involve far-away customers or suppliers.

Provinces vary markedly in soil quality, rainfall, and resource endowment. Within provinces, some counties are far more fertile than others, and individual communes vary in this respect as well. A strict policy of self-sufficiency would therefore permit some people to prosper mightily while others were condemned to harsh poverty. In practice, poor areas are subsidized and rich districts provide surpluses that are transferred to provincial or national authorities, who allocate aid to deficit provinces.

The concern for equalization has not prevented the authorities from channeling agricultural investments into the counties with the best conditions, where productivity gains will be maximized. The most barren districts are urged to follow the heroic example of Tachai, a commune in heavily eroded loess territory where millions of man-hours of work on check dams and terracing have built a model farm out of a wasteland. Self-reliant effort then justifies modest state subsidies, although major output growth is expected to come from fertile districts.

**Foreign trade**   Within its broad policy of economic self-sufficiency, China currently finds room for a modest amount of foreign trade. Its chief trading partners are its offshore neighbor, Japan, and its immediate neighbor, Hong Kong, along with other nearby Asian countries. Western Europe and North America now appear in China's diversified trade pattern also. China's chief exports are textile fibers, yarn, and fabrics; various foodstuffs; and a variety of raw materials. Its chief imports are ferrous and nonferrous metals, machinery and equipment, and various foodstuffs. This trade is useful in China's modernization efforts, but it is not a large and central feature of the country's economic development.

## CHINA'S DEVELOPMENT EXPERIENCE

The present Chinese economy reflects a strong traditional background as well as a violent sequence of major disruptions on the way to the current orderly situation. Here we examine China's historical background, the methods used to revolutionize the old society, and the economic sources of recent Chinese modernization.

**China's proud tradition**   The Chinese state system took shape some 2,200 years ago. Thereafter, despite several foreign invasions (the invaders were absorbed), an unbroken tradition prevailed. In literature, philosophy, and the arts, highly civilized forms were carried forward relatively unchanged until a century ago. Except during occasional periods of disunity, China was wealthy and powerful, dominating most of East Asia. Neighbors sent tribute to the Emperor of the Middle Kingdom. Pride, even arrogance, marked the Chinese attitude toward unknown nations on other continents.

In old China the patriarchal family formed the heart of a culture based on tradition. The child was trained to respect and revere his elders, including his ancestors. Models of propriety came from the past. Lines of authority came down strongly from old to young. Women played a very subordinate role. The individual typically lived as a disciplined member of a family group, submerging his or her own interests in the interests of the clan.

The principle of filial piety—respect for authority, age, and tradition—carried over into the organization of society. The Emperor stood at the head of a vast society in which each person had a proper position and role to play. Rules and standards for relations between the Emperor and his officials, and between officials and the masses, were based on ideals formulated many centuries earlier. Civil service examinations for the state bureaucracy upheld traditional precepts. Ritual and decorum defined "the right way" to behave for the individual family and the rulers of the state. Both looked to the past for guidance. Clearly, such institutions would prove stubbornly resistant to change.

The spread of European power forced China to give up her isolated grandeur. The last great dynasty of the Manchus (1644–1911) brought almost two centuries of domestic peace and prosperity, reaching a peak toward the end of the eighteenth century. But during the nineteenth century internal strains developed. Moreover, Western traders forced breaches in the Empire's trade controls; Western missionaries brought in, along with their Christianity, new ideas in science and government; and Western navies backed up these invasions with force. The proud Chinese were humiliated, the weakness of their state system exposed.

**Twentieth-century troubles: the rise of the communists**    The end of the Manchu dynasty in 1911 brought a weak Republic. Sun Yat-sen spoke for a new generation of Chinese, seeking a nationalist rebirth of China, using Western technology and political institutions. But the new regime could not control the whole country. The outer edges of the Empire fell away. In many areas, regional warlords ruled. In the late 1920s, Chiang Kai-shek emerged as the head of the Kuomintang Party, driving out its Community Party minority. Japan, having modernized rapidly in the preceding half-century, captured Manchuria from China in 1931 and invaded central China in 1937.

Meanwhile, Mao Tse-tung had led a disciplined remnant of

Chinese Communist disciples to a northwest provincial base, from which they gradually extended their power, patiently enlisting peasant support for overthrowing the old order. Party members led an ascetic life under strict discipline, fanatically dedicated to violent social change. New members were carefully trained in Mao's political doctrines and in methods of guerrilla warfare.

In order to hold back the Japanese, the Kuomintang and the Communists temporarily halted active hostilities in their contest for control of China, but after 1945 the civil war was renewed. In the face of United States efforts to arrange a coalition government, the Communists enveloped Manchuria and spread southeastward, isolating city after city. In 1949, Kuomintang forces were driven off the mainland, and on October 1, 1949, Mao's regime formally installed itself in power.

The preceding half-century of turbulence had not prevented the beginnings of industrialization in China's major port cities and in Manchuria. Western intervention brought with it the founding of a textile industry, coal mines, railroads, iron and steel works, and a modest range of other nonagricultural activities, accounting for perhaps 5 percent of Chinese output in 1937. Moreover, although average incomes in China were extremely low, they do not appear to have declined between 1900 and 1937. There was, in fact, a potentially available "surplus" above subsistence to be drawn on for investment in modernization. Under existing Chinese political and economic conditions however, this "surplus" was largely consumed by the well-to-do.

**The sequence of change in agriculture**  By 1949 the Chinese Communists had learned how to handle land reform. On gaining military control of an area, the party disarmed the landlords. A team of party members would then visit each village, get to know its people, and explain the party's definitions of "poor peasant," "middle peasant," "rich peasant," and "landlord." After a few weeks, public meetings would be held to redress grievances and to shift land from owners to tenants, with all villagers taking part under the skillful guidance of cadres. This revolutionary political transformation, which had spread over most of Mainland China by 1952, gave control of the land and its crops to the peasantry.

Peasant control, however, proved to be nominal because active Party cadres immediately began to promote mutual-aid arrangements under which several peasant households would join together in carrying out agricultural operations. Cost-reducing efficiencies were thus demonstrated. Later, increasing numbers of peasants were induced to join larger "agricultural production cooperatives," where further improvements were expected. The effort to create co-ops throughout the nation soon came to an end, mainly because the regime needed more grain for the cities and the army, and it was both unable to reorganize farm methods overnight and unwilling to invest heavily in agricultural modernization. In 1955, after a good harvest, the regime hastily acquired basic control over crop disposition by imposing the "collective farm" form, much as the Russians had done in 1929. Unlike their Soviet counterparts of 26 years earlier, the Chinese authorities achieved collectivization without also prompting a rebellious peasant reaction and thus were spared severe blows to agriculture of the kind dealt to Soviet farming in the 1930s (see Chapter 5). Then in 1958, after only two and a half years of the collective farm stage, the Party devised a still more drastic form, the agricultural commune.

**Party mastery of trade and industry**  Initially the private merchants and manufacturers of China were promised a large role in joint efforts with the new regime. Mao said, in June 1950, "The view held by some people that it is possible to eliminate capitalism and introduce socialism at an early date is wrong; it is not suitable to our national conditions."[2] In October 1951, however, a great drive was launched against "five vices" in private trade and industry: bribing of government personnel, tax evasion, theft of state property, cheating on government contracts, and stealing of economic information for private speculation. After nine months of investigation and denunciation, three-quarters of all private firms had been found guilty of various malpractices, enormous "fines" had been collected, and the independence of the business sector had been undermined.[3]

The regime succeeded at this time in halting the hyperinflation that had made the price level of August 1948, by one report, six million times the price level of August 1937. During 1950 the government curbed public expenditures, raised tax collections (especially the grain tax in kind), and pushed bond sales. In addition, the state acquired stocks of food, cloth, and other staples, holding

[2] *New China's Economic Achievements, 1949–1952* (Peking: Foreign Languages Press, 1952), p. 7.
[3] *Ibid.*, pp. 152–53.

them at regional centers for prompt shipment to any city or town where prices began to rise. This "goods intervention," together with a scheme linking salary payments and bank deposits to the price of a standard bundle of commodities, restored confidence in the currency. The presence of a scheme reassuring the public as to the purchasing power of its money paradoxically made the scheme unnecessary. Private banks were first put under state supervision, then combined into five state-private units, and finally, in December 1952, merged into a single system under the People's Bank.[4] Control of currency and bank deposits gave the regime strong leverage over all private activities.

The state also moved into trade and industry, setting up state trading agencies at many key points in the economy. These agencies bought food from the peasants and sold it to the public, preventing speculation and earning a markup. They acquired raw materials and contracted with processors for their fabrication, thus controlling manufacturing profits and retaining control over distribution of consumer goods through the state sales network. By 1957, China's businessmen and traders had been reduced in effect to state employees, shorn of all capacity for independent economic activity.

**Crusading morality** The Chinese Communists have made extensive use of vivid moral appeals in their drive for rapid change. The past is tied to all the evils of injustice, selfishness, and backwardness. The future, and the party's path to it, are seen in a blinding vision of equality, selfless service, and scientific progress. People know that the party has all the guns. But force can be held in reserve if persuasion produces voluntary consent. Who can defend a "reactionary" view forever?

Reeducation is carried out in small groups of six to a dozen co-workers or neighbors, led by a trained party activist. Small-group study has been used to change the outlook of city intellectuals and businessmen, to indoctrinate army recruits, and to keep party members up to the mark. Fellow-members bring tremendous psychological pressure to bear on the individual. Confessions and ideological autobiographies often reflect genuine, though perhaps brief, conversion. However, in 1957 a short period of free speech revealed that many converts retained their doubts; the authorities

---

[4] Choh-ming Li, *Economic Development of Communist China* (Berkeley: University of California Press, 1959), p. 146.

responded with renewed campaigns of reeducation. The most prolonged and intensive effort came with the Great Proletarian Cultural Revolution in 1965–69, when for four years Chairman Mao's supporters harangued and denounced all who seemed insufficiently committed to selfless service of the people.

The drive for rapid change has also made use of nationwide movements, short-run campaigns directed against specific problems. The "five-anti" movement against five business vices was an early example, as was the "three-anti" movement (against corruption, waste, and bureaucratic attitudes and practices in government offices) that accompanied it. There were mass movements for killing flies and sparrows in the cities; participation was required of everyone, young and old. The motto: "The people can do anything."

**The Chinese commune**   The Communist drive ran into economic and political difficulties in 1957, but the party, instead of easing its pressure, launched an all-out campaign in 1958 for still more rapid growth. There was to be a Great Leap Forward on all fronts. Both food and steel, both agricultural and industrial production, were to be doubled almost overnight.

The key to the Great Leap Forward was to be a new form of human organization, the commune. As originally imposed, its purpose (and effect) was to invade and dismantle the last remaining stronghold of freedom from party control—the Chinese family. When Chou En-lai, a chief lieutenant of Mao, was asked in the late 1940s what changes in Chinese life the party had in mind, he said: "We will make China over from a family-centered into a community-centered society."[5] Here, a decade later, was the means. An official source wrote, in September 1958:

> Since ancient times, peasants have treasured their homes, left them by their ancestors, above everything else. Now that private plots, houses, and part of one's livestock have come under commune ownership, all the ties that bind the peasant are broken. . . . The frames of individual families which had existed for thousands of years have been completely smashed.[6]

During mid-1958 the rural population was swept into some

[5] Albert Ravenholt, "People's Communes," American Universities Field Staff Letter, No. AR-8-'58, p. 14.
[6] Cited in Paul K. T. Sih, "The Chinese Communes," Thought Patterns, No. 7 (New York: St. John's University Press, 1960), p. 128.

26,000 giant communes; the new form of organization extended also to a large part of the urban population. Each commune contained from 5,000 to 65,000 people, typically around 25,000. The members lived like soldiers, organized in regiments, battalions, and companies. Work orders came from above, and all had to obey.

Commune labor was used for a mixture of farming and non-agricultural tasks. Members of city communes were sent on rural assignments, while farm communes mined local coal and smelted local iron ore or scrap. Great masses were shifted to irrigation or dam-building projects, especially during the off season. With commune mess halls set up to provide meals and nurseries established to take care of young children, some 120 million rural women were released to join in these tasks. In addition, both men and women got a stiff course of military training.

The movement, like earlier movements, went too far. At first normal family life was completely disrupted, men and women marching to separate work assignments, children to nurseries, and the elderly to old-people's homes. In places, overenthusiastic cadres tried to sweep all personal property into the commune and to keep people at work as much as twenty hours a day. By December 1958, however, the regime issued a resolution seeking to halt these excesses, and during 1959–61 a series of concessions restored a good deal of autonomy to the peasantry.

**Consequences of the commune**    For a few months the communes seemed miraculously successful. But wild claims for 1958 output increases were revised sharply downward in August 1959. Much of the so-called "steel" made in small backyard furnaces proved to be of very low quality. Although unusually favorable weather conditions helped produce what was clearly a record crop, and although Chinese agricultural exports to the USSR rose rapidly, crop estimates proved to be greatly exaggerated. Food shortages appeared in 1959 and grew worse in 1960, leading to desperate Chinese orders for food grains from Canada and Australia. What had gone wrong?

It now seems clear that the agricultural commune had been used as a massive instrument for extracting both work and output from the peasants, not through price and income inducements but through local administrative control. The peasants' small private plots were abolished, as were the local free markets where their produce was marketed. Where formerly peasants had been rewarded according to workdays put in, enthusiastic party cadres now sought to divide comune members' small returns according to need. The regime's stress on major crops forced a contraction in the time and effort peasants put into their numerous and important side activities of supplying a variety of goods and services to the general public.

Experience quickly showed the need to restrain the pressure of local cadres and find more effective means of inducement, but the adjustments were made with reluctance. As early as 1959 a semblance of free-market sales was readmitted. In 1960, peasants were urged to work again on private plots. In 1961, operating control was passed down from the commune management to "brigades" of two to three hundred households. In 1962, controls over crop choice and payment shares were delegated to even smaller "teams" of about forty households, corresponding roughly to the old pre-collectivization village. In this more relaxed and flexible form the commune stabilized in the mid-1960s as a workable combination of local autonomy and national coordination.

The Great Leap Forward in industry produced sharp output increases in 1958 and further gains in 1959, but after 1960 mounting difficulties led to a drastic fall in production. The collapse in agriculture reduced industry's raw material supplies. Overenthusiasm and misjudgment had wasted vast sums in unsound industrial investments. The policy of "walking on two legs"—producing manufactured goods both in modern large-scale factories and in small, primitive workshops—had proved impossible to coordinate and manage efficiently. Part of the Great Leap Forward had involved a shift of planning and plan-supervising authority from the center out to local authorities; this proved to be a serious error. Accurate data on performance were not coming in to the center, and interindustry coordination almost ceased. In factories, local party officials and overenthusiastic workers eroded normal management authority. Finally, in the summer of 1960, the Soviet engineers and technical advisors who had been helping build hundreds of projects left China suddenly, taking their blueprints with them. For all these reasons, industrial output fell by something like 40 percent in 1961.

From 1962 through 1965 the economy recovered rapidly, but in 1966 new political turmoil broke out with the Great Proletarian Cultural Revolution, directed against party leaders, government officials, industrial managers, and technical experts—all who threatened to become a new ruling elite like the old Chinese scholar-gentry class. Chairman Mao and Marshal Lin Piao led a fierce campaign against Liu Shao-chi and a majority of the bureaucracy, inciting attacks by teenage Red Guards and disrupting the cities for over three years. In places the army was called in to restore order. By mid-1969 a new structure of Revolutionary Committees replaced the old lines of control, and since then the economy has forged steadily ahead.

The early mass campaigns, the Great Leap Forward, and the Great Proletarian Cultural Revolution have served as drastic means for breaking out of the traditional institutional structure so firmly established in China. Each drive went too far. The authorities would concede, after a while, that excesses had been committed, and more reasonable arrangements would emerge. The process of change has thus been erratic; great spurts have been followed by breathing spells. It required two decades of tension and turbulence to bring the economy to its current peaceful state, and one cannot be sure that new convulsions do not lie ahead.

**Economic sources of modernization**    The spreading controls and massive drives of the 1950s permitted the new regime to carry through a basic reallocation of resources. From 1952 to 1958, output rose by something like 60 percent, but less than two-thirds of the added output was given to consumers. Instead, rationed consumption was made far more equal, incomes above the average were cut back, and the share of output going into capital plant and equipment was sharply increased. Taxes levied on agricultural produce, business activity, and consumer goods served to siphon off consumer purchasing power and finance state investment. Hundreds of new factories, power plants, rail lines, highways, dams, and irrigation works were built. Housing, schools, medical facilities, and social services were provided for the elderly and the destitute. Gradually the classical wealth and prosperity of the Middle Kingdom began to be restored, but this time with infusions of Western technology and with a radical leveling of individual incomes.

**The role of imported technology**    Another early source of industrial advance was the inflow of equipment and advisors from the USSR. The new regime moved rapidly in 1949 to seal off the

From *Chinese Literature No. 4 1975. Woodcut by Feng Chung-tieh.*

*New ways in an old setting*

mainland from the West. After June 1950, the United States also maintained an embargo and blockade along the Chinese coast. The new regime (in Mao's phrase) "leaned to one side," turning heavily to the USSR for imports, export markets, and developmental loans. Under formally negotiated agreements made in 1950, 1953, 1954, and 1956, the Chinese arranged to import all the equipment, together with blueprints and technicians, needed for some 211 major heavy industrial projects, forming the heart of the first Five-Year Plan.

These economic agreements between Communist China and the USSR included provisions for short-term credit to cover

Chinese imports, which grew rapidly until 1954, leveled off in 1955 and 1956, and fell in 1957. Chinese merchandise exports to the USSR, while running behind Chinese imports, also rose rapidly through 1956, when for the first time they slightly exceeded Chinese imports from the USSR. After a pause in 1957, both exports and imports rose sharply in 1958 and 1959; since then they have fallen off drastically. The trade deficit China accumulated during 1950–55 has been repaid painfully with interest, in spite of China's domestic difficulties.

Under the "lean to one side" policy, Russia rapidly came to account for over half of China's foreign trade by 1954, with other Communist bloc countries accounting for about one-fifth and the rest of the world about one-fourth. Thereafter, the Soviet share gradually declined, and in recent years China has made determined efforts to establish trade with nonbloc countries.

By 1965 China had paid for all the economic aid it received from the USSR during the 1950s and thus can be said to have laid the current burden directly on the Chinese people. Chinese exports of consumer goods (textiles and shoes, meat and rice, tobacco, fruits, and vegetables) imposed an immediate sacrifice in forgone consumption. At the same time this commodity trade, together with the services of some 10,800 Russian technicians who visited China, was a crucial element in China's initial efforts to industrialize. Imported machinery and equipment, embodying modern technology, provided an output-raising potential that greatly outweighed its short-run costs, especially as seen by the party. Without trade, many years of painful technological progress would have been required; with trade, traditional exports made possible the immediate acquisition of such capital equipment as modern electric power plants, steel mills, and truck factories.

**Organizing full employment**  China's reorganization of income flows was accompanied by changes in work organization that have served to enlist all labor power in productive activity. The new Chinese constitution follows the Soviet constitution in drawing on St. Paul's second epistle to the Thessalonians (2 Thess. 3:10) for the precept: "He who does not work, neither shall he eat." There is always something useful for everyone to do, and after more than a decade of intense experimentation, an effective system of rewards and penalties was worked out. Chinese administrators tell visitors that highly unequal rewards are not necessary to call forth steady enthusiastic effort. They assert that "equality fosters production." In rural teams and urban factories, one's fellow workers are all busy. Efforts produce visible results that are clearly making life better. It is thus difficult and unpopular to loaf. Local Revolutionary Committees encourage popular participation in arguments over methods of work and the sharing of results, all within the constraints of current party policies.

**Making use of intermediate technology**  A fourth aspect of China's approach to modernization concerns the way abundant labor is combined with scarce capital. Modern Western technology typically employs a large amount of capital equipment in proportion to its use of labor. Traditional Chinese technology typically combined simple wooden tools with large masses of labor. Crops grown and harvested by hand were carried to market by carrying pole, wheelbarrow, or sampan. As Western methods took root in treaty-port cities, textile mills, electric generating plants, and iron and steel works grafted Western factor proportions onto the edge of the Chinese economy. China now employs a very wide range of technology, running all the way from unchanged primitive methods to the production and assembly of electronic computers and nuclear weapons. In the 1950s China accepted Soviet stress on capital-intensive methods in heavy industry, but since then Chinese policy has consciously promoted the use of intermediate technology that can be applied in small-scale production units throughout the country. The equipment looks old-fashioned to Western eyes, and output per worker may be low by the standards of Detroit or Hamburg, but the proper comparison is with zero output from unemployed labor. The output to be shared increases, and the technology employed calls on all available hands to produce it. Muscles rather than machines were the motive power for China's traditional economy, and the transition to mechanical power is taking place only gradually. The Chinese do not seem to look down on traditional methods, and in fact give highly favorable publicity to peasant creativity in devising new ways to extend ancient practice.

This stress on intermediate technology is linked with a strong political principle that has colored Chinese economic affairs for the last decade. It is better to be "Red" than "expert." Advanced foreign technology is ideologically suspect. Capital-intensive methods, requiring advanced knowledge in the hands of a managerial elite, are seen as endangering the very purposes of Chinese development. During the Great Proletarian Culture Revolution, universities were closed down, research scientists were sent to learn from the peasants, and technical experts were scorned. It is, however, a safe guess that scientists and production engineers working on strategic weapons were protected from this drive, and major heavy industrial installations have continued their orthodox methods.

## CHINA'S OUTPUT EXPANSION: DRAMATIC BUT UNEVEN

The methods just described have produced marked increases in industrial production and moderate increases in agricultural output, although the economy has twice suffered serious setbacks.

The population has grown rapidly and massively, though it now appears that future growth will slow down. While the nature and extent of China's future growth are uncertain, analysis can at least clarify the prospects.

**The uneven record, 1952–74**    The general trend of Chinese output expansion since the first Five-Year Plan began in 1952 can be seen in Table 2-1 and Figure 2-1. For the first six years, agricultural output was raised slowly but steadily, while industrial output grew very rapidly indeed. By 1958, the gross national product as a whole had risen some 68 percent. The agricultural sector in 1958 turned out 30 percent more product than in 1952, and industrial production in 1959 was more than three and a half times as large as in 1952. The population, meanwhile, had grown by 15 percent, so that per capita GNP in 1958 was about 46 percent above its 1952 level. Agricultural output per person showed modest gains after 1954, while per capita industrial output climbed very rapidly to a 1959 level over three times what it had been in 1952.

The strains of the Great Leap Forward brought a sharp downturn in agricultural output after the bumper 1958 crop. Production dropped below 1952 levels in 1960 and 1961. After 1959, industrial production fell some 40 percent. As a whole, GNP in 1961 had dropped to a level only 22 percent above the 1952 starting point; per capita agricultural output had fallen to about 76

### TABLE 2-1
### Estimated Chinese Output and Population,
### by Year, 1952–1975
### Indexes with 1952 = 100

| | AGRICULTURAL | INDUSTRIAL | GROSS NATIONAL PRODUCT | POPULATION |
|---|---|---|---|---|
| 1952 | 100 | 100 | 100 | 100 |
| 1953 | 101 | 126 | 106 | 102 |
| 1954 | 101 | 147 | 111 | 105 |
| 1955 | 114 | 151 | 122 | 107 |
| 1956 | 117 | 184 | 132 | 110 |
| 1957 | 121 | 208 | 140 | 113 |
| 1958 | 130 | 302 | 168 | 115 |
| 1959 | 100 | 369 | 160 | 118 |
| 1960 | 94 | 384 | 159 | 120 |
| 1961 | 93 | 225 | 122 | 122 |
| 1962 | 111 | 238 | 139 | 124 |
| 1963 | 116 | 285 | 154 | 126 |
| 1964 | 127 | 339 | 175 | 128 |
| 1965 | 138 | 415 | 200 | 131 |
| 1966 | 139 | 481 | 216 | 134 |
| 1967 | 149 | 421 | 210 | 137 |
| 1968 | 139 | 463 | 212 | 140 |
| 1969 | 142 | 551 | 234 | 143 |
| 1970 | 156 | 653 | 267 | 147 |
| 1971 | 161 | 711 | 284 | 150 |
| 1972 | 157 | 772 | 295 | 154 |
| 1973 | 167 | 866 | 324 | 158 |
| 1974 | 170 | 901 | 334 | 162 |
| 1975 | 187 | 991 | 367 | 165 |

SOURCES: Derived from estimates compiled by Arthur G. Ashbrook, Jr., in U.S. Congress, Joint Economic Committee, *China: A Reassessment of the Economy* (Washington, D.C.: GPO, 1975), pp. 42–43. The preliminary 1975 output estimates are 10 percent over 1974 (see the *New York Times*, 22 Aug 75, p. 39), and the population figure is that of Table 2-2 (page 53).

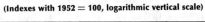

**FIG. 2-1**

**Estimated Output of the Chinese Economy,
by Year, 1952–1975**

(Indexes with 1952 = 100, logarithmic vertical scale)

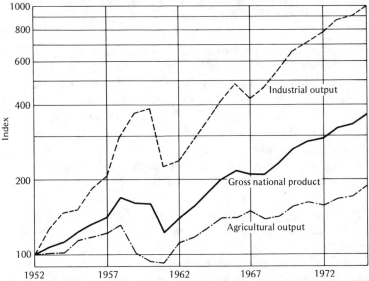

percent of the 1952 level; and although imports combined with rationing prevented mass starvation, there was widespread evidence of malnutrition.

From 1961 through 1966, the economy recovered rapidly and the GNP rose above its previous peak to more than twice the 1952 level. Again the expansion of industrial output went far beyond the rise in agricultural production; these indexes stood at 481 and 139, respectively. On a per capita basis, agricultural output more than regained the 1952 level and industrial output rose above the previous 1960 peak.

Once more, however, the economy was disrupted, this time by the political turbulence of the Great Proletarian Cultural Revolution, which caused a slight drop in agricultural production during 1968–69 and a sharper drop in industrial production during 1967–68. Overall, however, output fell by only about 3 percent, and since 1968 there has been rapid, steady expansion in GNP.

Over the whole period from 1952 through 1975, China's population has grown by about 65 percent. Agricultural production has just about kept pace in an overall sense, although this broadly parallel trend masks the much improved distribution of foodstuffs, which has brought an assured adequate diet to everyone. Industrial production per capita has risen to a level six times the 1952 figure, surely an impressive accomplishment.

**Rapid population growth**   The mid-1975 population of China appears to be about 942 million people, more than one-fifth of the world total. Two hundred years ago the figure was just over 200 million. Yet by today's standards the intervening growth was slow, as shown in Table 2-2. The death rate was only a few points below the birth rate, but the gradual, multiplied effect has been dramatic. Since 1950, Chinese population growth has been far more rapid. The evidence is not very precise, but Table 2-2 shows the most careful estimates available.[7] Total population grew from 550 to 942 million, with an average natural increase of 22 persons per thousand, primarily because of a marked fall in the death rate.

The Chinese census of 1953 revealed a larger population than expected, yet for a while China's leaders welcomed further rapid growth. Then birth control campaigns were launched, called off, and launched again. Eventually, a steady policy emerged under which early marriage is strongly discouraged (the approved age for marriage is 25 for women and 27 for men), and birth control information and equipment are very widely available. Family planning is seen as "aiding the emancipation of women, reducing their burden of housework and enabling them to devote more energy to various kinds of socialist constructive work." The authorities "combine state guidance with the free will of the masses. In our work we rely on the masses, mobilize the masses and make them carry out childbirth planning voluntarily and consciously."[8] This policy for densely populated areas is matched by a willing-

[7] Post-1957 population and output figures must be built out of fragmentary evidence, pieced together to form a consistent and plausible set of interlocked estimates. The output and population series used here are both on the high side, together implying plausible changes over time in per capita levels. For further discussion, see Leo Orleans' essay in U.S. Congress, Joint Economic Committee, *China: A Reassessment of the Economy* (Washington, 1975).
[8] "Speech of the Chinese Delegation at the International Conference on Population Planning For National Welfare and Development," Lahore, Pakistan, Sept. 25, 1973, pp. 4 and 6.

## TABLE 2-2
### Estimated Population of China, Selected Dates, 1750–2000, with Indicated Rates of Natural Increase

| YEAR | TOTAL POPULATION (in millions) | INTERVAL | AVERAGE ANNUAL NATURAL INCREASE PER THOUSAND |
|---|---|---|---|
| 1750 | 215 | 1750–1800 | 8.3 |
| 1800 | 325 | 1800–1850 | 5.6 |
| 1850 | 430 | 1850–1900 | 1.3 |
| 1900 | 460 | 1900–1950 | 3.6 |
| 1950 | 550 | 1950–1975 | 21.8 |
| 1975 | 942 | | |
| 1990[a] | 1146 | 1975–1990 | 17.0 |
| 1990[b] | 1322 | 1975–1990 | 22.5 |
| 1990[c] | 1518 | 1975–1990 | 27.7 |

1990 estimates: [a] low; [b] medium; [c] high.

SOURCES: The 1750–1950 estimates are from an unpublished paper by Michael Rodell and Holland Hunter, drawing on Aird, Durand, Ho, Perkins, Taeuber, and Thompson. The 1975–1990 midyear estimates are from John S. Aird, *Population Estimates for the People's Republic of China: 1953 to 1974* (International Population Reports, Series P-95, No. 73, Washington, D.C.: U.S. Department of Congress), February 1974, p. 23.

ness to foster rapid population growth in sparsely populated regions occupied by national minorities.

The potential for further growth in China's young population is very large in absolute terms, even if the birth rate is brought down quite rapidly. It looks as though the present population of almost 950 million people will rise by 1990 to somewhere between 1150 and 1500 million people, depending on trends in birth rates and death rates and assuming no catastrophic wars or natural disasters. The low estimate puts the current birth rate at 35 per thousand and the current death rate at 16 per thousand, and then projects gradual declines to 24 and 9, respectively, by 1990. The high projection has 1975 birth and death rates of 38 and 11 per thousand dropping to 34 and 6 by 1990. Thus, over the next 15 years China must find ways to take care of an addition to its population that will at least equal the present population of the United States and perhaps be more than twice as large.

**Prospects for output expansion**   Faced with these population growth prospects, what are China's chances of producing the necessary additional food and other kinds of output? The most basic factor conditioning China's capacity for expansion is her agricultural potential. So far, food supplies have kept pace with population growth; can the pace be continued?

On the physical side, the application of modern methods is generally seen as holding substantial promise, but only over a long period. Since the early 1950s, the Chinese have been working to renovate and improve the water control system of China, which was gravely weakened by a century of neglect. Problems of flood control, riverbed silting, and channel maintenance have been worsened by the soil erosion that followed removal of forest cover from the hills and mountains of central China. Since 1700 the growing population has pushed out of the old settled valleys and planted corn, Irish potatoes, sweet potatoes, peanuts, and beans where formerly a forest cover held the soil and ground water. The new regime has launched massive campaigns to reforest hills and mountainsides with seedlings, but it will necessarily take time for results to appear. Meanwhile, one must expect floods to continue.

The serious droughts that intermittently ruin crops in much of central and northern China cannot be prevented, although much can be done to offset their impact. Chinese peasant agriculture found ways over the centuries to fend off these blows, aided during the last century by modern means of getting food from surplus to deficit regions. But this requires adequate incentives and competent administration in the agricultural sector. Hasty and unwise irrigation of arable land has in some places hurt rather than helped crop yields; experience in many parts of the world now indicates that water management is far more intricate than is generally appreciated, and the Chinese evidently have much to learn.

Since 1960 the regime has shifted its emphasis from heavy industry to agriculture, under the slogan, "Agriculture as the foundation with industry as the leading factor." Industry is producing more agricultural implements than before and importing some fertilizer. Excess urban manpower has been redirected into agriculture, and greater initiative has been accorded the peasantry. It is too soon to say, though, whether the present compromise arrangements will stimulate sustained growth. With adequate investment, good morale, and modern techniques, it seems likely that agricultural output can continue to grow in China, despite its lack of much good additional arable land. If rising costs make additional domestic production difficult, China might have to turn to exporting other kinds of output in exchange for imported grain.

Prospects for expanding Chinese industrial production appear relatively unconstrained. The early view that China lacked resources for heavy industry has been abandoned in the face of exploration and discoveries, together with the cost-reducing impact of modern technology applied to resource extraction. For a quarter of a century the new regime has been building up a trained urban workforce on the small nucleus inherited from prerevolutionary days. In the countryside an inherited stock of handicraft skills has provided a base for the spread of intermediate technology. Along with this human capital, the stock of fixed plant and equipment has similarly grown in industry, transport, and the services sector as well as in agriculture. Thus the raw materials, labor, and capital necessary for output expansion are clearly obtainable. Recently, in fact, numerous oil fields have been opened up, and China has become a net exporter of oil which will thus be exchangeable for whatever China lacks. Major uncertainties arise, however, in the less tangible areas of motivation, morale, incentives, and the organization of complex activities.

**The clash between income leveling and output expansion**
China's agricultural and industrial output has been expanding in recent years on the basis of known, well-established technology. Local party activists have been able to stimulate the spread and use of technical knowledge held by the current generation of engineers and technicians. Managers and workers have evidently been creative and enthusiastic in putting present knowledge to work.

Differences in pay and perquisites between top management and unskilled workers are much narrower than in the West, yet morale and productivity have not been impaired. Recent Chinese policy has been founded on a deep conviction that a technological elite of "experts" is not needed for Chinese economic progress. Foreign science is suspect; the creative initiative of the masses is revered. Output growth adequate to match population growth may well require, however, that pay scales widen and differential rewards be offered to induce further technological progress after the present possibilities have been exhausted.

During the Great Proletarian Cultural Revolution, Chinese universities were closed and "experts" everywhere were denounced. Since then higher education has started up again, but ideology dominates science, and intellectuals remain cowed. Foreign visitors have been shocked by the evidence that active scientific inquiry has been quelled. Who will replace the present generation of Chinese scientists and engineers when they retire? Can a modern complex economy be built and prosper without an intellectual elite?

The conflict between equality and productivity has a geographic dimension as well. The expanded output required to meet the needs of several hundred million more Chinese may be obtainable only if efforts are concentrated in the most fertile and productive areas. A policy designed to raise poorly endowed regions to equality with the richest would surely yield smaller and slower output gains. So far, "investment in agriculture has most often been channeled into the naturally better-endowed areas where it would have the biggest impact on productivity, rather than into the poorer areas where it would help bring about a more equalized distribution of income."[7] It is clear, however, that China's leaders will continue to be challenged by the difficult problems of designing incentives and maintaining morale while transferring incomes from rich to poor districts.

## EVALUATING CHINA'S ECONOMIC PERFORMANCE

The first of our standards for measuring economic performance asks whether the economy provides amply for its people. Our answer in China's case must be relative. As we saw in Chapter 1, the Chinese standard of living is among the lowest in the world. Rural life is primitive by European or North American standards, and even the urban minority lives a very crowded and simple life compared to that of most people in rich countries. Compared, however, to China during 1900–1950, the present economy clearly provides a much better life for the bulk of the population. Public health and education have greatly improved, and an assured supply of food, shelter, and clothing has been established for all. Gross extremes of wealth have been cut away, and modest rations are equitably shared.

As for economic freedom, clearly the choices open to a Chinese citizen are nothing like those open to Europeans and Americans.

[7] Dwight H. Perkins, "An Economic Reappraisal," *Problems of Communism*, May 1973, p. 11.

The Chinese Communists have, in fact, gone far beyond the USSR in devising a totalitarian system in which centralized political decisions govern all economic activity. Peasants are not free to leave their villages, and urban youth are not free to choose their careers. People freely spend their modest incomes on a widening range of consumer goods but are subject to strong pressures for spartan simplicity. Decisions as to resource use, production methods, the composition of output, and investment patterns are all made through intense political procedures where party precept rather than individual welfare sets the standard.

The new China gets high marks for economic equity. It is unique among low-income societies in the extent to which it protects its poorest members against absolute penury. The helpless are provided for, and all who are able to work find useful tasks to perform. Moreover, modest rewards are perhaps more acceptable in the absence of extremely high incomes to provide painful contrasts.

Over the last quarter-century, China has provided a fair measure of economic stability in spite of intense periods of political instability. The Chinese people have been through convulsive changes in their personal lives but have been spared inflation, unemployment, famine, or other economic disasters.

China's record of economic growth has been marred by erratic spurts and slumps brought on by political struggle rather than by market forces. Recent years have seen steady, modest expansion, sufficient to raise output per capita by about 3 percent per year— not a high growth rate but still an impressive one. This growth has been obtained at the expense of individual freedoms most readers of this book value very highly. Chinese traditions are different, however, and perhaps Chinese modernization will continue in ways that draw only selectively on Western political forms and modern science to manage a vast collective society.

**SUGGESTED READINGS**

Eckstein, Alexander, Walter Galenson, and Ta-chung Liu, *Economic Trends in Communist China*. Chicago: Aldine Publishing Company, 1968.

> Twelve thorough, detailed analyses of the major sectors of the Chinese economy.

Lifton, Robert Jay, *Thought Reform and the Psychology of Totalism.* New York: Norton & Co., 1961.

Careful evaluation by a major American psychologist.

Prybyla, Jan S., *The Political Economy of Communist China.* Scranton, Pa. and New York: Intext Publishers, 1970.

Perceptive analysis by a thoughtful observer.

U.S. Congress, Joint Economic Committee. *People's Republic of China: An Economic Assessment.* Washington: GPO, 1972.

————, *China: A Reassessment of the Economy.* Washington: GPO, 1975.

Two wide-ranging, up-to-date collections of informed studies by specialists.

Students examining specific aspects of the Chinese economy will find useful and reliable material in *The China Quarterly* and the *Journal of Asian Studies.*

# INDIA 3

In 1947, after two centuries of British rule, India gained its independence. The new nation covered a territory as large as Europe, and its population, greater than that of Latin America and Africa combined, was made up of diverse religious and ethnic groups speaking a dozen major languages. India's quarter century of planned economic development shows both the strengths and the failings of mild, noncoercive efforts to raise the living standards of almost the poorest people in the world. Progress has been substantial but slow. Can the economy's performance be improved?

## THE BACKGROUND OF DEVELOPMENT

India is a land of great antiquity, achievements, and culture. But in recent centuries India has languished economically, and it is this recent background that sets limitations upon its present drive for development.

**The benefits inherited from British rule**  Perhaps the greatest service British colonial rulers rendered India was to bring about political unification. The British, through military conquest, gradually absorbed or dominated the hundreds of warring princely states; the resulting rule of law and order made commerce possible. The unifying force of English as the common government language and Urdu as the *lingua franca* of the army was considerable. But the real political unity of India came from the popular effort to win independence. The British gave the Indians a common enemy to unite against.

The British left behind them the ablest civil service of all the developing countries. While the colonial administration traditionally had used its civil servants primarily to collect taxes and maintain law and order, independent India redirected their energies toward planned economic growth. Without this corps of able officers, the government would not have been able to hold the country together and launch its development programs.

The British had introduced English education at an early period, with relatively good universities at the apex of the system. Indians thus were exposed to Western liberalism; they learned their lesson well and soon were calling for democratic self-rule. Although the spread of primary education was pitifully slow and technical education was neglected, the universities nevertheless provided India with better professional and civic leadership than most nations of its income level enjoyed.

Britain's primary interest in India was trade. A fairly advanced group of institutions, such as banks and insurance companies, had grown up to serve the business community and was ready to take part in the development of independent India. The best railroad system of South Asia had united the country's major regions.

**The problems inherited from British rule**   The British legacy thus provided India with a good base for economic development, but it also left obstacles in the way. One of these was a distrust of government. The British administration in India, founded in an era of laissez faire, was preoccupied with tax collection and law enforcement. This began to change about 1900, but as late as 1935 only 10 percent of government spending was for nation building or developmental purposes. Tax collection and police activities are unpopular under the best of circumstances and doubly so when administered by foreigners. Civil servants were therefore shunned and distrusted, even when they were Indians. This distrust of government survives today, especially in rural areas, and hampers central leadership toward national development.

Although Britain was without doubt the best colonial administrator of modern times, Indian development was directed toward British rather than Indian needs. Railroads were built to promote exports and imports, not to facilitate domestic economic development. Railroad building did not spur the growth of domestic steel and machinery industries, as it often has elsewhere, since equipment orders for rails and equipment were placed in Britain. Almost nowhere has industry developed without government subsidy and encouragement in its early years, but in India, except for public utilities, government pursued a hands-off policy. India's very low or zero tariffs permitted large imports of cheap British manufactured goods; Indian industry never had a chance to get started. As a result of these imports, Indian handicrafts declined, and artisans, notably the weavers, were forced to turn to agriculture. Ordinarily, as a country develops, the portion of the population in agriculture declines, but the reverse took place in India. In the fifty years preceding 1921, the part of the population relying on agriculture rose from about 65 percent to 75 percent; by 1951 it had receded only to 72 percent. This was not a healthy background for development.

**Indian values**     Much has been written of the materialism of the West and spiritualism of the East—probably too much. In India, one strand of religious tradition is symbolized by Lakshmi, the goddess of wealth; wealth and power are goals of life along with duty, liberation, and pleasure. Indians *are* willing to work for a higher standard of living. Yet another tradition calls for renunciation of material desires; the spiritual goal is to reduce one's claims on the physical world to a minimum. While economic achievement is valued by the typical Indian today, it is not placed as high in the hierarchy of goals in India as it is in the West. In particular, the ideal of renunciation checks the accumulation of savings.

In rural India the fatalism of the peasants blights the urge to change their miserable lot. The doctrine of *karma* says that a person's present station in life is the result of his or her behavior in previous incarnations and therefore cannot be changed. This of course undermines the incentive to raise one's position. Moreover, village tradition reserves each occupation for a particular caste, so there have been strong social barriers to upward mobility.

The extended family, including the grandparents and the families of all their married sons, which forms the basis of Indian social life, can diminish incentive to work. The lazy brother is cared for by the family; penury does not force him to work. The joint family provides more security than appears to be compatible with intensive economic effort. These considerations take the keen edge off the Indians' economic motivation but certainly do not nullify it.

# THE INDIAN ECONOMY BEFORE PLANNING

At the time it gained its independence, India was essentially an individualist economy, but mixed into the structure were a few public enterprises in utilities and railroads. The economy was a traditional one: poverty stricken, agricultural, and static. India's plight was sufficiently serious to discourage the most optimistic economic planner. Income per capita was below $100 a year, a level of poverty matched by few civilized countries. The nation was unable to put aside more than a pittance for physical and human capital formation; less than 5 percent of net national product was saved. The level of living had been virtually unchanged for a quarter of a century.

With a population of 360 million in 1951, India was badly overpopulated in relation to her resources. There was only four-fifths of an acre of cultivated land per person, and yields per acre were pitifully low. India's rice yield per acre was less than half that of China. The average diet was about 1,630 calories per day, or two-thirds of that required for health. Life expectancy at birth was 32 years; the debilitating effects of malaria reduced the energy of the workers, and epidemics of cholera, smallpox, and plague were common. Only 17 percent of the people were literate, and only 40 percent of the children were in primary school.

**Natural resources and agriculture**    India is rather well endowed with natural resources. It is true that the naturally fertile land has deteriorated through overuse and misuse, and that there is now little room to expand the cultivated area. But India has ample supplies of coal, iron, and other minerals, though not much oil or natural gas. Potential water resources both for irrigation and for power are relatively large.

India has been, and will long remain, an agricultural land. The progress in agriculture sets limits on the development possible throughout the economy as a whole. Methods of cultivation are labor intensive and extremely primitive. Ploughing is done with a wooden plough equipped with a small steel tip that scratches but does not turn the earth. Harvesting is traditionally done with a sickle only a few inches long, and cattle treading out the grain are a familiar sight. More depressing than technological backwardness is the peasantry's resistance to change. Farming methods condoned by generations of ignorance are sustained by fear of the risks of innovation.

Stagnation of mind and of technology was reinforced at the time of independence by the pattern of land tenure. Ownership of land was highly concentrated in the hands of a few landlords; the vast majority of the rural population were tenants or laborers. These latter groups had little to gain from increased production, so they had little incentive to increase their work or efficiency. In northern India the difference between rents charged the tenant and taxes paid the state left a very comfortable margin to land owners. The wealthier landlords became absentee owners, uninterested in agricultural progress and content to drain income from the countryside.

Inheritance laws combined with increasing population gradually reduced the size of holdings through subdivision until in 1951 the average size of an operated farm was 5.3 acres; 72 percent of the holdings were smaller than this. Even these tiny farms were fragmented into many plots scattered about the village, since each son wanted as his inheritance not just his share of the total land but his share of each field. Tenant farmers paid very high rents. When forced into debt by a bad year, peasants paid very high rates of interest. Millions became landless laborers existing precariously on the edge of starvation.

**Industry, commerce, and foreign trade**   The low productivity of Indian agriculture in 1950 was evident in the fact that the sector engaged 72 percent of the labor force but produced only 51 percent of the national income. Nonagricultural pursuits were more productive. In the small manufacturing sector, 16 percent of the national income was turned out by 11 percent of the labor force. The services sector, covering trade and finance, transport and communications, and government administration, produced a third of the national income while employing 17 percent of the labor force. But whereas commerce was relatively well developed, because turnover was quick and risk small, entrepreneurs hesitated to enter manufacturing, where capital investment is larger and returns are realized only over a longer period. Of the 15 million workers in mining and manufacturing, only 3 million were in factories; most of the others were employed in handicrafts and cottage industry. Those workers in what might be called modern industry were only 2 percent of the working force; they produced only 6 percent of the national income. India is a large subcontinent, and as long as the economy remained static, it could exist with a minimum of outside contact. However, the British had built up a thriving trade in which India supplied raw materials and some textiles in return for manufactured products. By 1951, food production had fallen behind population growth, so food grains were the most important single import item. To pay for these, India exported cotton and jute textiles, tea, hides and skins, vegetable oils, spices, and a number of other raw materials. The large food imports made it difficult for India to export enough to pay for all its imports.

## INDIA'S PLANNING EXPERIENCE

The first four years following independence were spent primarily in establishing law and order and settling political problems. A constitution was hammered out on Western lines. Several hundred princely states were absorbed into the Indian Union and the maharajas were pensioned off. Coincident with independence, the subcontinent was partitioned, and Pakistan was created as a new state. For a year India and Pakistan were at war over the control of Kashmir. Although Mahatma Gandhi, the prophet of independence, was a man of peace, India was born in violence. It is little wonder that economic planning for the future was put off a few years.

**The first Five-Year Plan, 1951–55**  In 1951, the first Five-Year Plan for economic development was launched to cover the period from April 1, 1951 through March 31, 1956.[1] The first Plan rested on the view that India was too poor to rely on the slow, unplanned development process followed by Britain and America. The way of life depicted in the Hollywood movies shown in Indian towns made many people impatient for immediate progress. Communists were exploiting the discontent born of poverty; India could not afford the luxury of slow development that a less harried age had permitted the West. Therefore, Prime Minister

[1] India's fiscal year begins on April 1 and thus includes portions of two calendar years, but for brevity we shall refer to each year by its major portion. For example, "1974" will mean the fiscal year April 1, 1974 through March 31, 1975.

Nehru's administration decided to quicken the pace of development by government action. Individual voluntary savings would be supplemented by forced public savings through taxation, and the government itself would establish some industrial enterprises. The intent was to stimulate economic development through increasing governmental leadership and participation in the economy.

The problems facing India were so enormous, however, that the first Plan was put together very cautiously. The planners cut the suit to fit the available cloth. First, they added up the financial resources the country could afford from taxes, domestic saving, deficit financing, and foreign aid. This set the level of their possible investment. On the basis of their best information, they then assumed a capital–output ratio of 3 to 1, meaning that each net investment of three units would increase the output stream permanently by one unit. In addition, they assumed that 20 percent of each addition to income would be saved and reinvested; thus, an engine of growth would be established. The planners then estimated what results they might reasonably expect, and these became the goals of the Plan.

The basic objective was to restore full production and lay a firm foundation for rapid future development. Specifically, the government hoped to increase national income by 11 percent over the five years, food grain output by 14 percent, and finished steel production by 70 percent (in 1951, steel production was minimal); to raise the proportion of children of primary school age in school from 42 to 60 percent; and to achieve a series of other similar targets. Since nearly three-quarters of the people depended on agriculture for a livelihood, and since food is the basic need of any desperately poor population, agriculture was given first place in the plan. Food production was to be increased through the use of fertilizer, large irrigation projects, and a mass program of teaching farmers modern techniques. However, the government did not put much effort into increasing industrial output; this was left to the private sector.

In a country like India, as agriculture goes, so goes the nation. In the last years of the Plan, unusually good monsoons caused crop production to soar; this caused prices to fall somewhat and made it easier for the government to pursue its development projects without inflation. By the end of the Plan in early 1956, total real national income had risen 18 percent and per capita income 11 percent; net investment had risen from 5 percent to over 7 percent of national income. The major goals had been fully or nearly achieved: food grains had increased by 22 percent instead of the expected 14 percent, steel and coal had fallen a little below target, but iron ore had exceeded expectations. Fifty percent of the children of primary school age were in school. Everyone felt elated that India had at last begun to move ahead.

**The second Five-Year Plan, 1956–60**   It was in a mood of optimism that the second Plan was drawn up. The sights of the nation were lifted; national income was to be raised 25 percent by 1961, or almost 5 percent a year. There was to be rapid industrialization, with the government taking a decisive lead in heavy industry. Eight million new nonagricultural jobs were to be created to absorb some of the discontented unemployed and thus reduce income inequalities. Within these overall goals, a number of specific targets were set, including increasing production of food grains an additional 22 percent, irrigated acreage 23 percent, electric power capacity 88 percent, steel production 231 percent, and the proportion of primary-school age children in school 10 percentage points (from 50 percent to 60 percent).

To achieve all this, effort had to increase sharply. Government outlay was to be more than doubled in the second Plan, $9.6 billion as compared to $4.1 billion in the first. Net investment was expected to rise from 7 to almost 11 percent of national income. Taxes, especially excise taxes, which burden the poor, would have to be raised substantially. Unwilling to raise taxes more drastically, the planners proposed to finance 30 percent of the development cost by public borrowing, another 25 percent through credit creation by the central bank, and 17 percent from foreign aid. Critics warned of the inflationary and foreign exchange dangers of such methods, but the Plan proceeded.

The emphasis in the second Plan was shifted from agriculture to industry, as indicated in Table 3-1. The planners decided to follow the Soviet example of focusing on heavy industrial expansion rather than letting the demand for producers' goods grow slowly in the train of increasing consumer demand. The "socialist pattern" of society became the watchword. While private industry was still encouraged, public enterprise was expected to dominate most of the expansion in heavy industry.

It was not long before the economy began showing strains,

## TABLE 3-1
## Indian Government Development Outlays, by Sector,
## First through Fourth Five-Year Plans
## (in percent shares)

| SECTOR | FIRST PLAN | SECOND PLAN[a] | THIRD PLAN[a] | FOURTH PLAN |
|---|---|---|---|---|
| Agriculture and irrigation | 31 | 22 (19) | 20 (21) | 22 |
| Industry, mining, and power | 19 | 27 (34) | 39 (37) | 36 |
| Transportation and communications | 24 | 29 (21) | 17 (24) | 10 |
| Social services | 26 | 22 (26) | 24 (18) | 32 |

[a] Figures in parentheses show percent shares based on actual outlays during the period.

SOURCES: Government of India, Planning Commission, *Second Five-Year Plan*, pp. 51–2; John P. Lewis, *Quiet Crisis in India*, p. 81; *The Economic Weekly*, November 14, 1964, p. 1823.

largely because of three miscalculations of the planners. (1) They had underestimated the need for capital equipment imports both in the public sector and for the expansion of private industry; by 1957, foreign exchange balances were running low. (2) Food import requirements had been underestimated; the small crop in 1957 called for large imports of grain if people were not to starve. (3) Population was growing faster than the planners had expected, and this increased the need to import food. The result was that food imports used up scarce foreign exchange, making necessary sharp cutbacks in imports of capital equipment. The private sector, particularly, was denied licenses to import machinery. The entire growth mechanism ground to a standstill; inflation set in, but real national income stopped growing.

Articles in the Western press compared the Indian effort unfavorably with that of China. Friends of India feared Communist inroads if India failed to make substantial progress. The "Aid-to-India Club" (the United States, Britain, Canada, West Germany, Japan, and the International Bank for Reconstruction and Development) supplied emergency credits of about $700 million, enabling India to import capital equipment once again. This infused life into the growth process; good weather brought a bumper crop in 1958, and growth picked up once more. The final year of the plan period saw sharp gains in both agriculture and industry.

Still, the targets of the second Plan were not fully met. Real national income rose about 20 percent rather than the 25 percent hoped for. The number of new jobs created outside agriculture fell short of the target by over one million. Nevertheless, the advances of the last year overcame the effects of the 1957–58 crisis, and most key targets were from two-thirds to four-fifths fulfilled. Grain production increased about 17 percent, steel output 120 percent; 60 percent of the children of primary school age were in school.

**The third Five-Year Plan, 1961–65**  Of the problems that faced India's policy makers as they approached the third Plan, two were most pressing: population growth and inflation. Rapid population growth meant that agricultural production, especially of food-stuffs, had to be increased significantly. Added numbers also meant that unemployment and its attendant discontent might exceed allowable bounds unless strong efforts were made to provide jobs for the growing work force. Because the heavy deficit financing of the second Plan had contributed materially to steady and worrisome inflation, the planners felt that borrowing from the central bank should no longer be relied on to augment financial resources for the Plan.

The major goals for the third Plan were: (1) to raise national income by 5.5 percent a year, or 31 percent over the five years; (2) to reach self-sufficiency in food grains by raising their output by at least one-third; (3) to lay a base for heavy industrial self-sufficiency in another decade or so by raising coal output 76 percent, steel output 160 percent, and electric power capacity 120 percent; and (4) to further income equality by creating 10.5 million new nonagricultural jobs and getting 76 percent of the primary-school age children into school.

The Plan called for raising investment from the 1960 rate of 11 percent to over 14 percent of national income by 1965, and for raising savings from 8 percent to 11 percent of national income, even while relying on generous foreign aid. Higher taxes were scheduled, though the plan expected four-fifths of the increment in national income to go into consumption. As Table 3-1 indicates, the third Five-Year Plan intended to shift government development expenditures still more toward industry by comparison with actual allocations during the second-Plan period, while keeping agriculture's share about the same and reducing the proportion of the total going to transportation and communications. The actual rate of output expansion during the third-Plan period was lower than under the second Plan. After a slow start, the third and fourth years were good ones, but in 1965 the monsoon failed and national income dropped by 5 percent. Renewed brief conflict with Pakistan caused a temporary halt in Western aid shipments; this in turn checked industrial expansion. The government had drafted a fourth Five-Year Plan but deferred its adoption until prospects could be more firmly estimated. For the three years 1966, 1967, and 1968, interim annual plans gave expression to government policies. These were the difficult circumstances under which Indira Gandhi, Nehru's daughter, became Prime Minister.

**The three interim years, 1966–68**    In 1966 the monsoon failed again, and only emergency imports of food grains from the West saved India from famine. Agricultural shortfalls brought industrial growth to a halt and set off sharp rises in both wholesale and retail prices. Fortunately, 1967 was a bumper agricultural year and 1968 was almost as good, so the economy recovered rapidly. Industrial production resumed its upward course and the cost of living stopped rising. The government felt justified in accepting a somewhat scaled-down set of targets for the fourth Five-Year Plan to cover the years 1969–73.

**The fourth Five-Year Plan, 1969–73**    The fourth Plan was fairly optimistic, calling for a growth of national income averaging 5.5 percent annually, including 5 percent for agriculture and 9 percent for industry. The Plan stressed the need to reduce dependence on aid from abroad and the need to reduce economic inequalities. Without marked shifts in the structure of Plan outlays, the planners expected through a large number of concrete practical programs to improve the efficiency of economic activity, while directing its fruits a little more equitably toward the "weaker sections" of society.

Achievements during the fourth-Plan period once again fell short of Plan targets. The first two years went well, but agriculture faltered in 1971 and serious drought brought a marked fall in 1972. The final year saw recovery, but the average annual growth rate in national income was barely 3 percent instead of 5.5 percent. The cost of oil and other imports had risen sharply and, although India benefited from higher world prices for some of its exports, on balance the changes in world trade dealt India a serious blow. Domestic shortages again generated inflationary pressures that increased political tensions and complicated economic policies. Social programs were cut, as efforts focused on measures to raise industrial and agricultural production.

A draft of a fifth Five-Year Plan was issued in 1973, reflecting the strong political position of Indira Gandhi's administration and the continued optimism of the Planning Commission. It puts major stress on programs to foster development for the bottom third of the population, find ways to start the birth rate downward, reorganize agriculture for greater productivity, and stimulate renewed industrial expansion. Current events suggest that these targets will be very hard to reach, and in fact that a revised final plan with more modest targets may be necessary.

This economic record is summarized in Table 3-2 and Figure 3-1. The impact of weather on Indian agriculture stands out clearly in the graph, as does the steady growth of industry. Comparison of columns 1 and 4 in Table 3-2 shows that, except for the years 1957, 1964, and 1965, agricultural output growth stayed ahead of population growth. What were the policies that both shaped and responded to this record?

## INDIAN DEVELOPMENT POLICIES AND PROBLEMS

India's experience under national economic plans, covering the period from 1951 through 1975, provides a valuable record of democratic planning in action. As we have seen, the government has responded to the very difficult problems it has faced by applying a series of gradually changing policies. Here we comment on these policies before going on to evaluate India's performance and weigh its prospects.

**Evolutionary or revolutionary transformation?** The Government of India is a federal union of states reflecting the country's great diversity. Its leaders have deliberately chosen to build upon

## TABLE 3-2
## Indian Output and Population, by Year, 1952–75
### Indexes with 1952 = 100

| YEAR | AGRICULTURAL OUTPUT | INDUSTRIAL OUTPUT | NET DOMESTIC PRODUCT | POPULATION |
|------|---------------------|-------------------|----------------------|------------|
| 1952 | 100 | 100 | 100 | 100 |
| 1953 | 108 | 104 | 106 | 102 |
| 1954 | 109 | 108 | 109 | 104 |
| 1955 | 109 | 111 | 111 | 106 |
| 1956 | 114 | 116 | 116 | 108 |
| 1957 | 109 | 118 | 115 | 110 |
| 1958 | 121 | 119 | 123 | 112 |
| 1959 | 120 | 125 | 126 | 115 |
| 1960 | 128 | 134 | 135 | 117 |
| 1961 | 128 | 140 | 139 | 120 |
| 1962 | 126 | 146 | 141 | 122 |
| 1963 | 130 | 154 | 148 | 125 |
| 1964 | 142 | 160 | 160 | 128 |
| 1965 | 124 | 163 | 152 | 131 |
| 1966 | 127 | 166 | 156 | 134 |
| 1967 | 151 | 172 | 172 | 137 |
| 1968 | 154 | 180 | 177 | 140 |
| 1969 | 165 | 191 | 188 | 143 |
| 1970 | 176 | 199 | 198 | 146 |
| 1971 | 177 | 206 | 203 | 149 |
| 1972 | 174 | 217 | 206 | 152 |
| 1973 | 190 | 219 | 212 | 156 |
| 1974 | 187 | 224 | 214 | 160 |
| 1975 | 196 | 235 | 225 | 164 |

SOURCES: Output indexes derived from Government of India, Central Statistical Organization, *Estimates of National Income and Product* (1971), *Estimates of National Product, Saving, and Capital Formation* (1973), and (for 1972–74), "Quick Estimates of National Income" (January 1975). The preliminary 1975 output estimates are 5 percent over 1974 (see *The New York Times*, October 26, 1975, p. 12). The population index is derived from an absolute series using Government of India, *Economic Survey, 1973–74*, figures for 1956 and 1961–73, plus United Nations, *Demographic Yearbook 1970*, estimates for 1952–55 and 1957–60, raised to fit the 1956 and 1961 Government of India benchmarks.

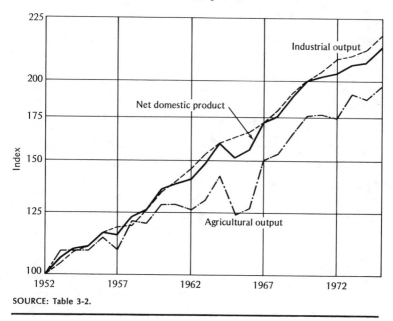

**FIG. 3-1**

**Output of the Indian Economy, by Year, 1952–1975**

(Indexes with 1952 = 100, logarithmic vertical scale)

Industrial output

Net domestic product

Agricultural output

SOURCE: Table 3-2.

this varied background and let the new society evolve gradually out of the old. The constitution identifies the welfare of the individual as the goal of society, and at both federal and state levels contending interests struggle to define the common good. The freedom of its citizens has been held essential to their welfare, so Indian constitutional processes have been built upon the British model, with some borrowing from that of the United States. Economic development, therefore, has proceeded within the limitations set by a democratic and rather decentralized political framework. Economic modernization has occurred through persuasion rather than force.

**Public or private initiative for development?** For more than twenty years the Government of India has sought to spur economic development without itself having control of very much economic activity. It called in 1954 for a "socialist pattern" of society, a phrase that has come to mean two things. First, it signifies an intention to reduce the extreme economic and social inequalities that have been inherited from the past. Through legislation and exhortation the government has sought to reduce the harsh discrimination embedded in the caste system. To help the mass of poor peasants, land reform programs have sought to transfer land to the landless. India's evolutionary approach is seen in the compensation paid to landlords and in the relatively large holdings they have been allowed to keep. Other moves toward equality have included establishment of a small social security system for some workers, encouragement of collective bargaining by trade unions, and efforts to provide jobs for the unemployed.

Second, the "socialist pattern" has meant that the government seeks an increasing share of ownership or control of heavy industry. At the same time, however, private industry has been encouraged to grow. Existing private industry has not been nationalized (although fourteen large banks were taken over in 1969–71), but the 1956 Industrial Policy Resolution called for some industries to be expanded primarily by government. Heavy industry of basic and strategic importance, public utilities, and activities requiring state aid have grown primarily with government support. Development in fields outside a specific list of twenty-nine industries has been left to private enterprise.

To date, change in both these respects has been modest. Caste distinctions still shape Indian village life, and glaring income inequalities still exist. The shift toward public ownership has been negligible. Between 1951 and 1970, the output of public enterprise increased only from 3 percent to about 7 percent of national product, and government's total contribution to net national product increased only from 7.6 percent to 14.8 percent. In the United States, government controls nearly twice this proportion of income; one can hardly say that India is far along the socialist road.

India's government directly controls only its own expenditures and those of government-run activities. It can influence private business decisions through persuasion, tax inducements, tariff policy, import licenses, and building permits. Thus, while the government plans for the whole economy, the plans are followed only in the public sector. The "plan" for the private sector is largely a guess as to how private farmers, tradesmen, and business-men will act.

The planners are finding it hard to change the traditional investment pattern in India. Under each of the first three Plans, public investment fell short of expectations, while private business expansion proceeded considerably more rapidly than anticipated. With some 85 percent of production still in private hands, success in meeting Plan targets lies largely with private enterprise. Therefore, private investment remains a key factor in India's development.

**Financing development**    Most Indians are so poor that all their meager income goes into consumption. Paying for a funeral or wedding drives them into debt, while a bumper harvest enables them to put silver bracelets on their wives. People and businesses outside agriculture, however, can and do save, putting funds into land or other income-earning assets. The private sector has financed its additions to plant, equipment, and working capital fairly readily by plowing back profits and floating securities on the organized stock and bond markets of Calcutta, Bombay, and New Delhi. Public-sector finance has been more difficult.

Voluntary saving by the public has provided more than one-third of the resources for public investment. The government has been pleased with the public's response to bond sales. In the future, the government would like to tap the fairly large non-monetized savings of prosperous farmers, now put into jewelry or used to bid up the price of land, neither of which adds to productive resources. Efforts are being pushed to establish and popularize a network of rural institutions for small savings to mobilize these hoardings for productive use.

Taxation is another means for shifting current resources from consumption into public-sector capital formation. But India's rate of taxation has been one of the lowest in the world: in 1951, taxes took only 8 percent of the national income, and this increased to only 10.2 percent in 1960. By 1972 the fraction had risen to 16.7 percent, but most developed countries siphon off over 25 percent of the national income in taxes. India's tax receipts have gone mainly into current expenditures, leaving little to finance public investment.

The recurring conflicts with Pakistan and the Chinese invasion of 1962 have added materially to India's development problems.

After the early struggle over Kashmir, the share of defense out-lays in the central government budget fell steadily from 30 percent in 1952 to 15 percent in 1959–61. The Chinese incursion in 1962 caused a rapid rise in defense spending from 3.1 billion rupees in 1961 to 8.2 billion (25 percent of the budget) in 1963. Defense outlays fell slightly in 1964 but since then have grown steadily, taking between 19 percent and 22 percent of the central budget. The 1971 defense outlay of 12.4 billion rupees was about 21 percent of the government budget and 3.5 percent of that year's net national product. The share seems small, but the re-sources involved could spur development if they could be shifted.

India's efforts to finance economic development have been complicated by several periods of serious inflation, reflecting poor crops, war, or deficit financing. At first, good weather helped, and the 1956 cost of living was no higher than at the start of the first Plan. After 1956, the general consumer price index rose at the modest rate of 3.5 percent per year to 1963. Over the next four years, however, the cost of living rose rapidly at about 12 percent per year, reflecting a brief war with Pakistan in 1965 and bad harvests in 1965 and 1966. Those who gained from these higher prices did not, in general, invest in growth-promoting projects nor were their gains taxed away.

The government chose not to shift resources from private con-sumption into public investment by deficit-induced increases in the money supply that would feed inflation and bring about "forced saving." Instead, the earlier practice of covering as much as a third of public investment by borrowing from the central bank was restrained; during 1961–65, deficit financing accounted for 13.2 percent of Third-Plan outlays. In 1966–68 the fraction fell to 10.1 percent, and the fourth Plan intended that it fall to 5.3 percent. With good harvests and budget restraint, the con-sumer price index again rose modestly from 1967 through 1972 at about 3.2 percent per year. Recently, however, a number of factors have been pushing prices up; in 1973–74 prices rose by 20 percent annually, and inflation again became a major problem.

**Foreign trade and external assistance**　In order to modernize and expand its industrial base, India has been importing a large volume of machinery and other industrial equipment for twenty years. Imports of oil have steadily increased, and at times large imports of food grains have been necessary. India's exports, however, have not been sufficient to cover all her imports, and export growth has been sluggish, reflecting two difficult aspects of the outside world. First, world demand for India's tea, jute, and similar primary products, has been growing very slowly. Second, Indian efforts to export manufactured goods have faced very stiff competition from Japan, West Germany, and other developed nations. Indian producers have not been notably enterprising in keeping up to date with innovations that lower costs and raise quality.

Few countries in the early stage of development have been able to export enough to pay for the imports that spur their development. The United States for many decades relied on British and European loans. India since the mid-1950s has similarly relied on foreign financial assistance. The amounts that India had utilized by the end of 1973 came to the dollar equivalent of almost $20 billion. Seventy percent was in loans requiring repayment; 20 percent was in the form of commodity aid (mostly grain), and 6 percent came in the form of grants not requiring repayment. The United States has been the biggest lender, but the USSR, West Germany, the United Kingdom, Japan, and a dozen other countries have participated along with international institutions. Interest payments on outstanding debt now offset more than half of each year's new borrowing. Greater self-reliance is a major objective of Indian policy, but prospects make it clear that continued borrowing will be necessary for a long while.

Indian imports of food grains have usually supplied about 5 percent of India's needs. As a result of two successive bad monsoons, food grain imports accounted for 14 percent of India's grain supply in 1966 and 12 percent in 1967. The import share dropped below 1 percent in 1972 but has since risen again. Typically, food purchases from abroad account for about one-sixth of India's outlays on imports, but the fraction varies considerably; it rose to one-quarter in 1966 and fell to one-twentieth in 1972. If India could become self-sufficient in food, valuable foreign exchange would be released for other purposes.

The drastic rise in oil prices since 1973 has dealt a major blow to the Indian economy. Just before the change, imports of petroleum (and fertilizers largely based on petroleum) were taking about 19 percent of India's expenditures on imports. Since India is now forced to pay more than three times as much as before for these key inputs into both agriculture and industry, it may have to devote as much as half its future outlays on imports to oil and petroleum-based products.

**Transforming Indian agriculture** In spite of over twenty years of governmental efforts, India's traditional farming methods have not yet been decisively altered. During the first decade, "community development blocks" reached a small fraction of India's peasant villages, and better practices were demonstrated. During the second decade, an Intensive Agricultural District Program focused on the more fertile areas, introducing improved high-yield seeds, together with fertilizer, water, and insecticides. In some districts progress was substantial, but vast regions of backwardness remain.

The "green revolution" that has been so effective for wheat in Mexico and rice in the Philippines gave a major boost to Indian agriculture in the late 1960s. The new strains of wheat proved especially useful in the northwestern and western parts of the country. "Miracle rice" has been less successful, and coarse grains have not yet been affected, but overall agricultural output was pushed up at least 20 percent. These high-yield varieties require abundant fertilizer, water, and insecticides. They permit two or even three crops a year if inputs are applied promptly and the harvest is quickly removed and stored. Unfortunately, it is not the poor farmer but the well-to-do landowner who can finance these off-farm inputs, master the new technology, and organize the new procedures. The social impact of the "green revolution" in the countryside, therefore, has been unsettling, with the benefits accruing to the upper layers of the population while those at the bottom suffer further displacement. Drought in 1972 cut the harvest by some 9 percent, and fertilizer shortages combined with sharply higher oil prices to thwart further progress in 1973–74, but monsoon rains in 1975 were good and the grain harvest rose to a new high.

Although India can still extend somewhat the area of land under cultivation, the addition of 10 million people each year to the rural population steadily reduces land availability per person. How can these additional millions earn a living? Half of them are in households with less than five acres of arable land, and a quarter are in households with no land at all. In issuing the fourth Five-Year Plan, in 1970, the Planning Commission gave special attention to the problem and proposed a number of programs "to enable as large a section of the rural population as possible, including the small cultivator, the farmer in dry areas and the agricultural labourer, to participate in development and share its benefits."[2] One program was to help small farmers in highly productive areas get the financial credit and training that would make their small tracts viable. Another effort focused on cooperative farming, but the Planning Commission stated frankly that "problems of motivation and organization met with in this approach have not yet been successfully solved on any significant scale."[3] A third direction involved schemes for rural roadbuilding, construction of irrigation works, and other forms of social overhead capital, using unemployed local labor paid with central funds or paid in kind with food grains supplied under U.S. Public Law 480 ("Food for Peace") or subsequent aid programs. Finally, numerous efforts to develop nonagricultural job opportunities were expected to relieve some of the pressure on the land. The overall problem nevertheless grew steadily worse during 1970–75.

**India's population problem**   As we have seen, India is already overpopulated in relation to its agricultural base and present level of technology. India must feed each person from less than three-quarters of an acre; by contrast, the United States uses about 2.3 acres of cultivated land per person. The average U.S. farm is 400 acres while India's is 5 acres. With added capital and improved technology, India can raise output per person, but the fewer the additional people, the higher the per capita output will be.

Rapid population growth in an already overpopulated country makes higher incomes much harder to achieve. With limited foreign exchange, if food must be imported, machinery imports must be cut, so industrial growth is hurt. The presence of millions of young people raises the need for investment in housing, school buildings, and other forms of social capital. The problems of reorganizing society to provide food and jobs for additional millions of people become much more difficult to solve quickly and peacefully.

The fearsome fact is that India's population growth has been speeding up, from roughly 1.9 percent annually in the 1950s to 2.3 percent in the 1970s, since death rates have fallen markedly

[2] See Government of India, Planning Commission, *Fourth Five-Year Plan*, 1969–74 (1970), pp. 120 and 149–56.
[3] *Ibid.*, pp. 22 and 214–32.

and birth rates have not. Even if the birth rate now begins to fall, the number of women entering childbearing age is so large that total births will continue rising for at least two decades.

The Government of India launched a family-planning program in 1952 and has gradually put increasing stress on lowering the birth rate. Efforts have included the widespread dissemination of information about family planning, distribution of contraceptive devices, and encouragement of voluntary sterilization. The program has shown some success, mainly in urban areas, but the drive lost momentum in the early 1970s and currently lacks clear direction. Government channels for communication and control are not able to persuade very many Indian couples in the villages that small families would be in their own interest, or to provide adequate contraceptive supplies to those who are persuaded.

**Personal and regional inequalities**   India fits under the general rule that the economic development process does not reach the bottom part of society for a long time. In spite of concern expressed in the first Indian Five-Year Plan and continued recognition of the problem, the bottom third of the population is not appreciably better off now than it was a quarter of a century ago. The Planning Commission estimates that in 1973 the poorest 30 percent of the people received only 13 percent of national disposable consumption income; their per capita income is pitifully low. These 150 million people fall into several groups: small farmers in dry or mountainous areas, landless peasants in crowded areas, and the urban poor. They are unproductive because they lack land and tools, suffer from ill health, and lack even rudimentary education. They are unemployed or underemployed, and their number has been growing.

How can the development process be brought to these groups? The Government of India is pursuing several strategies. In areas of intensively irrigated agriculture, some workers can be employed in ancillary tasks. In some areas, animal husbandry (livestock and chicken raising) can be pushed. Skills in weaving and handicrafts can be developed. Programs for construction of low-cost rural housing, irrigation works, rural roads, schools, and clinics can employ many thousands. Small-scale manufacturing operations can be scattered through the countryside. Efforts are under way in all these areas.

The growth of commerce, industry, and services is everywhere associated with the growth of cities. Millions of poverty-stricken peasants are drawn to India's cities; the largest cities have long been swamped by masses of unemployed, and medium-sized cities now face the same pressure. Nineteenth-century European and American cities had jobs for most of their new arrivals, but late twentieth-century manufacturing processes can increase output with far less than proportionate increases in labor, so those displaced from agriculture now are not easily absorbed by cities. Uncontrolled city growth also leads to enormous capital gains for a few as urban land rises in value. The draft of the Fifth Plan of the Government of India shows keen awareness of these problems but sees as yet no clear solutions.

The bottom third of the Indian population are scarcely touched by education. India has worked hard to raise the degree of literacy and provide at least rudimentary education for all children of school age. Unfortunately, too much money and manpower has gone into university-level education, producing an oversupply of college graduates, while not enough has gone to the elementary level, especially in regions where the least advanced groups reside. In tribal areas and rural villages, less than half the children between six and eleven complete four years of primary school. The mass education effort is costly, in teachers, buildings, supplies, and travel expenses. When educational funds are cut, the cuts fall here.

**Initiative, controls, and organization**   Since the mid-1960s, there has been slack in the Indian economy, reflected in both unemployment of labor and underutilization of capital capacity. The country has been caught in a vicious circle. Domestic purchasing power is not large enough to create a vigorous demand for current production; this in turn discourages producers from making the outlays on labor and other inputs that would increase current purchasing power. Exports have not been a source of stimulus for the Indian economy. In this situation, business and government leaders have clashed over ways to initiate a forward drive.

The government has learned that mere controls cannot induce development. It has put ceiling prices on food grains in order to protect the urban poor and has placed rigid controls on imports from abroad in order to support the input needs of high-priority projects. But when grain purchase prices are too low, farmers are discouraged from growing more and are reluctant to sell to government procurement agencies. Artificially low interest rates have encouraged technological choices that substitute capital for labor, while an artifically high value for the rupee until 1966 encouraged imports and discouraged domestic production.

Indian businessmen have responded alertly to profitable market opportunities, but these opportunities have arisen chiefly among the urban, modernizing minority with purchasing power—not in traditional villages. Left to itself, therefore, private industry might expand briskly, leaving the great mass of the rural peasantry even further behind. Large landowners, in turn, may respond again to the profit possibilities that lie in "green revolution" agricultural technology, but do so by using capital-intensive methods without employing much more labor. Government officials are sensitive to the plight of the poor but lack the power to organize major new programs.

In recent years food shortages, renewed inflation, industrial stagnation, corruption in government, and private speculation in grain markets have put severe strains on India's governmental processes. A democratic government subjected to sharply con-

Wijesoma/Ceylon Observer. From *Atlas World Press Review*, October 1975.

flicting views that reflect deeply opposed vested interests, ethnic friction, and interregional rivalry, has great difficulty in working out an acceptable and effective set of economic policies, Mrs. Gandhi's emergency measures in mid-1975—throttling the press, jailing hundreds of opponents, and manipulating parliament—appeared to some a desperate attempt to control the situation. Current reports indicating an improved food outlook, sharply reduced inflation, and successful campaigns against corruption suggest that the immediate crisis may have passed. Grave political and economic problems remain, however, and only time can show how they will be solved.

## A COMPARATIVE EVALUATION

India and China, the two most populous societies on earth, are neighboring Asian giants with deeply different institutions for organizing their economic activity. Each is in a desperate race to keep output growth ahead of population growth. Here we compare their experiences to date and offer an evaluation of India's performance.

**The growth record**   When India and China started their Five-Year Plans in the early 1950s, their per capita incomes were about the same and their prospects for development seemed roughly comparable. Since then, as we saw in Chapter 2, drastic changes in China's institutions have brought the economy forward along a path marked by sharp ups and downs. The collapse of the Great Leap Forward brought a drop of over 25 percent in Chinese total output, and the strains of the Great Proletarian Cultural Revolution caused another fall of perhaps 3 percent in 1967–68. Nevertheless, the level of Chinese GNP in 1975 was about 3.7 times the 1952 level. India's mild institutional changes have brought far steadier progress, and more than doubled her net domestic product over the same period, though without matching the Chinese output expansion of the last six years. The sketchy evidence now available does not permit thorough analysis, but it is both interesting and important to compare these two contrasting records and speculate on the factors that lie behind the contrasts.

One key difference between India and China lies in their treatment of the agricultural sector. India has made no drastic organizational changes, and although year-to-year gains in output have been somewhat precarious, gradual progress has been made and agricultural output has almost doubled since 1952. China, on the other hand, squeezed the peasantry during 1953–57, drove them unmercifully during 1958–59, and reaped disaster during 1959–61 when drought and floods combined with rural disorganization to lower agricultural output by more than 25 percent. Since 1962, farm production has recovered and expanded in China, so that by 1975 it appears to have reached a level about 80 percent above the 1952 starting base. Thus, in agriculture the contrast is between gradual Indian progress and drastic Chinese efforts that have only recently achieved substantial gains.

Indian industrial output has grown slowly but steadily by over 100 percent during this period. Chinese industrial output has expanded far more rapidly, rising almost tenfold, but, as shown in Chapter 2, the growth process has been marred by convulsive spurts and setbacks.

From 1952 through 1975 the two populations have grown at about the same rate—each rising by roughly 65 percent, at an average annual rate of 2.2 percent. In both countries, women of child-bearing age make up a large share of the total female population and the potential for further population growth is very great. As we have seen, China's efforts to lower the birth rate have recently been more strenuous than India's; their impact on Chinese population growth has not yet been appreciable but it now appears that in the next decade China's birth rate will decline more rapidly than India's.

The interaction of these output and population trends in both countries is depicted in Figure 3-2. The top panel shows that, in total output per capita, India moved slowly forward for the first twelve years, through 1964, reaching a level close to that of the post-Leap recovery in China. Then two bad monsoons and a war with Pakistan set India back, while China moved ahead. India's recovery and subsequent expansion raised per capita output only very modestly. China was set back by political turbulence after 1965 but recovered vigorously after 1968, so that by 1975 the index of Chinese total output per capita (1952 = 100) reached 222, compared to India's 137. The average annual rate of expansion in total output per capita over this whole 23-year period was 3.5 percent for China and 1.4 percent for India.

This result incorporates very different patterns in agriculture and industry. The second panel in Figure 3-2 shows that Indian agricultural output growth has stayed somewhat ahead of population growth so that agricultural output per capita fell below the 1952 level in only three years. In China, however, ten of the twenty-three years were below the starting point, and even recently there has been no appreciable rise in per capita agricultural output over the level of twenty years ago. India's average annual growth rate here has been 0.80 percent, while China's has been 0.53 percent. It should be stressed, however, that the distribution of food among the Chinese people has been systematically managed to assure a basic minimum to all. In marked contrast, the overall progress in Indian per capita agricultural output masks a distribution system that leaves millions of people close to starvation.

The bottom panel of Figure 3-2 presents a vivid contrast between the steady but unspectacular rise of Indian industrial output per capita and the rapid though sharply fluctuating expansion of China's industrial output. On average, the per capita output of China's industrial sector has risen 8.1 percent per year; the rate for India has been 1.6 percent. Chinese authorities, having established a secure floor for popular welfare at an austere level, have channeled resources into cumulative expansion of industrial production. The Government of India, with similar intentions but far less vigor, has not been able to induce similar results.

**Evaluating India's performance**     India's record is that of a predominantly market economy in which agricultural and most non-agricultural activity is in private hands, although the government makes strong efforts to guide the course of economic development. How shall we assess its performance according to our five standards? Let us take them in order.

At a very low level of development, India cannot provide plenty for its citizens. It has been generating steady increments of output, but income distribution is highly unequal and the gains from output expansion have not reached the bottom third of the population. In this respect, China's performance has been superior.

As for economic freedom, the ability to choose one's job, one's place of residence, and one's pattern of consumption, the Government of India imposes few restrictions, but for most Indians these choices are sharply limited by the constraints of poverty. A person who lacks earning power or a backlog of assets cannot exert much economic freedom. For those above the median, however, India offers all the basic economic freedoms of a market economy. The contrast with China provides food for thought.

**FIG. 3-2**

**Total, Agricultural, and Industrial Output
Per Capita, India and China, by Year,
1952–75**

(Indexes with 1952 = 100, logarithmic vertical scale)

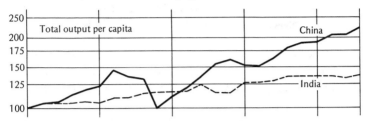

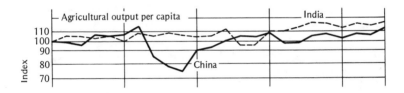

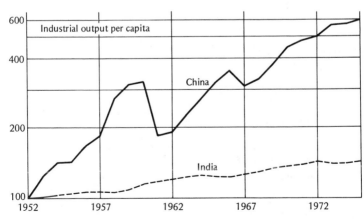

SOURCE: Derived from Tables 2-1 and 3-2.

Equality of opportunity is officially present in India under laws calling for equal treatment of all, regardless of religion, caste, or color. Actual opportunities are harshly limited by the poverty that produces malnourished, ill-educated citizens, often without access to land or the other resources that enable people to be productive. Middle class and wealthy Indians now have wideranging opportunities, though women still find only a few occupations open to them and racial exclusiveness informally restricts entry to many trades. Caste barriers are weakening, however, especially in the cities, and skills are being developed in the expanding nonagricultural labor force. Education is raising the sights of millions of young people. Again, comparisons with China deserve reflection.

India's record in economic stability is relatively good, compared to that of most other low-income developing societies. Neither runaway inflation nor catastrophic mismanagement has disrupted the economic environment. Agriculture depends precariously on weather conditions, however, and Indians cannot feel secure when the threat of famine is still hovering over the future.

Finally, the test of adequate output growth is one that India passes, say, with a C+. Given her problems, and starting from her initial situation, she has made impressive progress. But output has not grown fast enough to raise living standards decisively or to build a solid foundation for future prosperity.

**SUGGESTED READINGS**

Chen, Kuan-I and J. S. Uppal, *Comparative Development of India and China*. New York: Free Press, 1971.

> An organized selection of 33 detailed papers covering the record through 1969.

Government of India, Planning Commission, *The Five-Year Plan*, 1952; *The Second Five-Year Plan*, 1956; *Third Five-Year Plan*, 1961; *Fourth Five-Year Plan, 1969–74*, 1970; and *Draft Fifth Five-Year Plan, 1974–79*, Vols. I and II, 1973. New Delhi: Government Printing Office and Controller of Publications.

> Basic statements of government intentions and past performance.

Lewis, John P., *Quiet Crisis in India*. Washington: Brookings Institution, 1962.

An informed review, both sympathetic and critical.

Malenbaum, Wilfred, *Modern India's Economy: Two Decades of Planned Growth*. Columbus, Ohio: Merrill Publishing, 1971.

Critical analysis by a development economist.

# MEXICO

4

Centuries ago, Mexico was host to the remarkably sophisticated Aztec civilization. Subsequently it fell into deep poverty, aggravated by harsh political tyranny. Reborn (so to speak) through revolution in 1911, Mexico has moved at first slowly, then with increasing rapidity, toward equality with the world's affluent economies. Just as importantly, after many decades of laboring under the huge shadow of its North American neighbor, the United States, Mexico is in all important respects coming into its own. And it is doing so without transforming the economy into a command system. The federal government (which has been for several decades the preserve of a single political party with wide public support) in many ways influences but in no genuine sense dominates the private entrepreneurs who own and control the bulk of the nation's resources. Mexico's problems are many, but both its short- and long-term prospects are bright.

## ECONOMIC STRUCTURE AND ORGANIZATION

**Resources**  In physical terms Mexico is a medium-sized country. Its nearly two million square kilometers (roughly 770,000 square miles) makes it much smaller than the USSR, the United States, or China, and only two-thirds as big as India, but four times the size of France and much larger than the other members of the European Community. Its territory varies from tropical rain forest to arid plateau, and most of it is usable (or potentially so) for human purposes. The country is comparatively well endowed with natural resources, notably petroleum and natural gas, coal, and a variety of ores. Where rainfall is inadequate, irrigation is feasible. Mexico's forests are large and its coastal waters supply abundant fishing resources.

Compared to the United States, the European Community, and the USSR, Mexico has a modest stock of social overhead and directly productive capital. Yet it is anything but impoverished in this respect. The transportation sector, for instance, includes 46 merchant vessels, well over one million passenger cars, about 600,000 commercial motor vehicles, nearly 23,000 miles of railway track, and 40,000 miles of paved roads. The educational system is similarly extensive; in addition to a nationwide network of primary and secondary schools, there are 51 universities (of which 34 are state-supported) and 13 teacher-training schools (of which seven are public). And, as we shall see shortly, the stock of capital in the extractive and manufacturing sectors is growing steadily.

Mexico's human resources are at once its most valuable asset and its growing liability. On the one hand, the population is overwhelmingly youthful and thus has its most productive years before it. The median age of all Mexicans is barely 15; only 4 percent of the populace is age 65 or older. Health conditions are improving rapidly: Life expectancy at birth, which has reached nearly 60 years for males and 63 years for females, is fast approaching equality with the rich economies; and the crude death rate fell from 25.6 per thousand in 1930–34 to 9.2 per thousand in 1970. Upwards of two-thirds of those of working age are literate, with a similar fraction of 5–14 year olds enrolled in school.

The major source of difficulty in Mexico's demographic situation is the exceedingly rapid growth of its population, a growth that has accelerated over the last few decades. The death rate, as noted, has fallen by 64 percent since 1930–34. But the birth rate has diminished only slightly, falling from 44.5 per thousand total population in 1930–34 to 42.1 in 1970. The natural rate of increase, therefore, *rose* from 1.9 percent in the earlier period to 3.5 percent currently. If the present rate of growth persists, Mexico's population, 60 million in mid-1975, will reach 140 million by the year 2000. Then as now, more than half its citizens will be under age 15 and thus dependent upon others for their livelihood. And then as now the nation's policy makers will need to find ways to generate opportunities for gainful employment for an ever-growing labor force.

**Changing structure of employment and output**   Mexico's progress in economic development is mirrored in the employment and output estimates of Table 4-1. More than half the labor force

## TABLE 4-1
### Mexican Labor Force and Output, by Sector, Selected Years, 1940–70

#### LABOR FORCE
(thousands of men and women)

| YEAR | AGRICULTURE | INDUSTRY | SERVICES | TOTAL |
|---|---|---|---|---|
| 1940 | 3,831 | 747 | 1,340 | 5,918 |
| 1950 | 4,824 | 1,319 | 2,202 | 8,345 |
| 1960 | 6,086 | 2,131 | 3,036 | 11,253 |
| 1970 | 5,284 | 2,798 | 4,932 | 13,014 |

#### Percent Shares

| | | | | |
|---|---|---|---|---|
| 1940 | 64.7 | 12.6 | 22.7 | 100.0 |
| 1950 | 57.8 | 15.8 | 26.4 | 100.0 |
| 1960 | 54.1 | 18.9 | 27.0 | 100.0 |
| 1970 | 40.6 | 21.5 | 37.9 | 100.0 |

#### GROSS DOMESTIC PRODUCT
(billions of pesos at 1960 prices)

| | | | | |
|---|---|---|---|---|
| 1940 | 9.2 | 12.7 | 24.2 | 46.1 |
| 1950 | 16.0 | 23.6 | 48.5 | 88.1 |
| 1960 | 24.4 | 46.6 | 89.2 | 160.2 |
| 1970 | 34.5 | 102.2 | 159.9 | 296.6 |

#### Percent Shares

| | | | | |
|---|---|---|---|---|
| 1940 | 20.0 | 27.5 | 52.5 | 100.0 |
| 1950 | 18.2 | 26.8 | 55.0 | 100.0 |
| 1960 | 15.2 | 29.1 | 55.7 | 100.0 |
| 1970 | 11.6 | 34.5 | 53.9 | 100.0 |

SOURCES: Derived from estimates in Clark W. Reynolds, *The Mexican Economy* (New Haven: Yale University Press, 1970), pp. 386 and 371–73; International Labor Office, *Yearbook of Labor Statistics 1973* (Geneva, 1973), p. 75.

is still engaged in agriculture, but while this sector held 65 percent of the labor force in 1940, its share has fallen to about 50 percent today. Over the same period the industrial sector of the economy raised its share of the labor force from one-eighth to one-fifth. The output produced by the agricultural sector, however, made up only 20 percent of Mexican gross domestic product in 1940 and the fraction has fallen to about 12 percent today, thus illustrating the disproportionately low productivity of labor in agriculture. Labor in industry, on the other hand, contributes more than its share to the nation's output; here a fifth of the labor force generates over a third of the gross domestic product. In the services sector, which covers commerce and finance, the professions, transportation and communications, and civil servants (as well as street sweepers, shoe shiners, porters, etc.), about one-fourth of the labor force accounts for just over half of total output.

*Agriculture*  Although agriculture has declined in relative importance both as an employer of labor and in share of national income generated, it is and will continue indefinitely to be a large, relatively prosperous sector, especially in this new era of global food shortages. Mexico produces a sizable portion of its own agricultural consumption requirements; and its exports of agricultural output—notably, fresh fruits and vegetables, beef cattle, honey, sugar, and cotton—account for nearly half the total value of its sales abroad.

The most distinctive feature of Mexican agriculture is the land tenure system. Based on a "functional theory of property" embedded in the Constitution of 1917, the system is grounded upon the proposition that "The Nation shall at all times have the right to impose on private property such limitations as the public interest may require as well as the right to regulate the enjoyment of natural resources which are susceptible of appropriation, in order to make an equitable distribution of public wealth and to care for its conservation." Article 27 of the Constitution provides specifically "for the division of large landed estates; for the development of small agricultural holdings under exploitation; for the erection of new centers of rural population with the lands and waters which may be indispensable to them; for the development of agriculture and for avoiding the destruction of natural resources and the damages which property may suffer to the prejudice of society."

Under this doctrine, ownership of property by private persons is subjected to a variety of conditions and public proscriptions. Most importantly for present purposes, Article 27 afforded the bases for the dissolution of huge prerevolutionary *haciendas* (private estates) and the institution of a large-scale land-reform program. In particular, the functional theory of property has been applied to the *ejido*, a semicommunal village organization. Lands donated to an *ejido* belong to the village, which is forbidden to sell, mortgage, or lease the land. If the *ejido* is of the individual type, as is usually the case, the village must distribute cultivable portions among the farmers who will work them. The farmers are not permitted to hire labor, and the land assigned to them reverts to the village if they fail to utilize it for two successive years. The Mexican government has also sponsored the larger cooperative *ejido*, which involves farmer-participants in collective effort and mutual sharing of output, typically commercial crops produced in volume through application of relatively large amounts of capital equipment.

Grants of land to *ejidos* began as early as 1915 during the presidency of Venustiano Carranza. They have continued ever since, amounting to more than 23 million hectares,[1] or nearly 57 million acres, during the presidency (1964–70) of Gustavo Diaz Ordaz. All told, on the order of half of Mexico's total agricultural area of 169 million hectares is occupied by *ejidatarios* (members of ejidos), the great majority of them owner–operators. Less than 2 percent of total agricultural holdings, representing about 10 percent of aggregate farming area, are operated under the collective system. In contrast, the census of 1910 showed fewer than 11,000 *hacendados* (estate-holders) controlling some 57 percent of the national territory, and of this number 834 held 1,300,000 square kilometers. One hacienda owner possessed properties equal in size to all of Costa Rica. At the other end of the scale, some 15 million persons were landless.[2]

Data pertaining to the productivity of Mexican agriculture are scanty and unreliable. Scraps of evidence suggest strongly that the output/input ratio is comparatively low, largely because of adverse climatic and soil conditions: only 12 percent of the land is tillable, less than 8 percent is actually cultivated, close to 80 percent of cultivated land gets insufficient rainfall, and about three-fourths of crop failures are attributable to lack of rain. The national government has addressed these difficulties in two ways. First, a 1946 amendment to the Constitution enlarged the standard grant of land, setting it at 10 hectares if the land is regularly watered, 20 hectares if it is not. Second, nearly all of the government's investments in agriculture in recent years have been for

[1] One hectare = 2.471 acres.
[2] Morris Singer, *Growth, Equality, and the Mexican Experience* (Austin and London: Published by University of Texas Press for the Institute of Latin American Studies, 1969), p. 56.

large irrigation projects, to the benefit of more than 3 million hectares of land under cultivation.

A major and as yet unsettled question is whether agricultural efficiency has been sacrificed at the altar of the small individual *ejido*. In Mexico, as elsewhere, it is argued that economies of scale can be realized in a farming collective, provided it is well organized and well managed. The validity of this contention cannot be adequately tested, in part because the collectives have suffered from poor management and inadequate organization and in part because very few of Mexico's farmers have been willing to be part of a collective, thus severely limiting the latter's number.

*Industry*  Defined by convention to include mining, petroleum, manufacturing, and electric power, the industrial sector has grown markedly since 1940. In a period when real gross domestic product was advancing rapidly, this sector's share of aggregate output rose from about 25 percent in 1940 to more than 34 percent currently. And whereas less than 13 percent of the country's labor force was employed in industry in 1940, the figure was roughly 23 percent by the early 1970s.

In considerable part, the industrial sector's growth reflects expansion in various manufacturing industries. The development of manufactures has not only reduced Mexico's dependence upon imports of manufactured consumers' and producers' goods, it has also contributed importantly to the development of an export market and consequent generation of foreign exchange. Among Mexican manufactured exports that are price- and quality-competitive in the world's markets are chemical and rubber products, automotive parts, textiles, copper and steel tubing, electrical equipment, wood and metal furniture, and typewriters. The list is certain to expand in years to come.

In outward appearance, the industrial sector is firmly but not entirely in the hands of private enterprises, some of them sprawling conglomerates. It is indeed true that more than 80 percent of the total value of industrial output originates in privately owned and operated concerns. But the Mexican government's role in industry is substantial. Numerous industries near or on the economy's "commanding heights" have been nationalized, including the railroads, the airlines and airports, the maritime fleet and harbor and port facilities, petroleum extraction and refining, radio and telegraph systems, and electric power. The federal government also owns and controls portions of such industries as sugar refining, iron and steel, cement, fertilizers, chemicals, motor-vehicle assembly, and railway-car manufacturing. Like other economies in the East and West, it invests large sums annually in construction of low-rent housing, highways, health-care facilities, and educational institutions. And through a mixture of monetary, fiscal, commercial, and direct regulatory policies it profoundly influences the pricing, production, distribution, and investment policies of all nominally private industrial enterprises.

These observations must not be construed as an assertion that the flow of power, authority, and influence is one-way, from government acting independently to passive industrialists large and small. True, for several decades Mexico has been ruled by a single political party that has elected Presidents constitutionally endowed with far more freedom of action than their counterparts in the United States. The political leaders are keenly aware, however, that they need the support of key industrialists and take care to satisfy the latter's essential needs and demands. To recite the old adage, one hand washes the other.

*Petroleum*   The development of the Mexican economy, like others the world over, owes much to extensive use of relatively inexpensive energy produced from fossil fuels, especially petroleum. Unlike many countries—notably, the members of the European Community and Japan—Mexico has substantial oil deposits within its own boundaries. Originally exploited by foreign concessionaires from Britain and the United States, the Mexican properties were nationalized in 1938, provoking a brief but very unpleasant diplomatic crisis. Confounding earlier pessimism about its ability to manage the industry, the state-owned monopoly enterprise Petróleo Mexicano (Pemex for short) has become the largest company in Latin America, with over 70,000 employees, $3 billion in assets, and output that supplies more than nine-tenths of Mexico's domestic consumption. Its near-future prospects, and thus those of Mexico's economy, are even brighter because a new oil field was discovered in southern Mexico in 1974. The size of the find is uncertain but has been estimated at up to 20 billion barrels, which would make it, in the words of Pemex's director, "the richest yet in the country." At the least, the newly found pool will make Mexico totally self-sufficient in petroleum for some years to come and also enable it to profit handsomely from sales abroad at prices that, since 1973, are several times higher than ever before.

**Foreign trade** Mexico's economic health and growth depend in considerable measure upon the vigor of its trading relations with the outside world. As is common among economies at its stage of development, Mexico is currently importing more goods and services than it exports, and the deficit on current account has grown noticeably in the last decade or so. Concurrently, the composition of both exports and imports has been changing. While agricultural, forestry, and mineral products remain important, accounting for about half the total value of exports, their share has declined markedly in favor of manufactured goods, foreign (chiefly U.S.) visitors, and sales of goods and services along the Mexican–United States frontier. And whereas previously Mexico was a heavy buyer of consumers' goods from abroad, a rapidly growing share of its imports are raw materials and producers' goods.

The geographical distribution of Mexico's external trade has also shifted in recent years, although it continues to be heavily dependent upon the United States for both exports and imports. Specifically, the U.S. at present buys approximately two-thirds of Mexico's exports (versus 90 percent in 1940) and supplies about 62 percent of Mexico's imports (versus nearly 80 percent in 1940). Europe's share of Mexican exports has risen from 5 percent to about 13 percent, and its share of imports has grown from 14 percent to upwards of 30 percent. Still small but beginning to increase noticeably is Mexican trade with other Latin American economies, a development that reflects the end of the era in which the area's countries had limited bases for trade because they produced highly similar products.

What makes these shifts in the composition of trade especially remarkable is that they occurred during a period when Mexico's terms of trade (the relationship between import prices and export prices) were steadily worsening. Between 1950 and 1970 the import-price index increased on the order of 150 percent, whereas the export-price index rose less than 50 percent. The prospects in the foreseeable future, as we shall note later, are somewhat better.

**Regional characteristics** Regional inequality in income and employment is a fact of life in Mexico as much as it is in India, Europe, and most of the rest of the world. In part, the differences reflect uneven interregional distribution in the quantity and quality of resources; land is not equally fertile in each region, commerce and industry tend to cluster together, etc. Moreover, governmental policies have accentuated differentials in regional rates of development; for example, conscious of the latent political power of urbanites, the government has held down food prices in the cities and thereby held back the growth of rural incomes. Political considerations, coupled with population pressure in urban areas, have led the government to assign the bulk of its outlays on civil works, education, and the like to the cities at the expense of the rural regions. The Federal District and the North Pacific region, as a result, have progressed far more rapidly than the north central, central and southern regions. Redress of regional inequalities is not yet high on the national agenda but probably will be in the near future.

**Economic institutions**  In Mexico the main device for allocating resources and distributing incomes is the pricing mechanism. This is true not only in the country's major industrial and commercial centers but also in those rural districts still characterized by "penny capitalism." Under penny capitalism, "There are no machines, no factories, no co-ops, or corporations. Every man [with his family] is his own firm and works ruggedly for himself. Money there is, in small denominations; trade there is, with what men carry on their backs; free entrepreneurs, the impersonal market place, competition—these are in the rural economy."[3]

The organization of the remainder of the economy, however, is far removed from the pure *laissez-faire* model. The state intervenes pervasively. Not only are the utilities (railroads, electric power, etc.) publicly owned and operated, but their resale prices are commonly fixed, not to cover long-run costs, but to promote attainment of other objectives, such as expansion of certain kinds of industrial output. Restrictions upon commerce with the rest of the world have been liberally imposed, notably to stimulate domestic production of substitutes for imports and thereby both to conserve foreign exchange and to generate growth in domestic income and employment. Great sums, as noted earlier, have been

[3] Sol Tax, *Penny Capitalism*, Smithsonian Institution, Institute of Social Anthropology, Publication No. 16 (Washington, D.C.: Government Printing Office, 1953), p. x.

expended from the public treasury to enlarge the infrastructure. And a network of national banking institutions, headed by the Banco de México and Nacional Financiera, provide financing for private and public enterprises whose activities are judged to be important to the nation's well-being.

## ECONOMIC DEVELOPMENT

Beginning in 1821, when Mexico regained its independence after three centuries of Spanish rule, the Mexican economy passed through four stages, each of which can be roughly dated: 1821–76, the post-independence phase; 1877–1911, the Porfirian era; 1911–40, the Revolutionary period; and 1940 to the present, the rapid-growth stage. The characteristics of each period deserve at least brief review because, as Shakespeare put it, "The past is prologue."

**Independence to 1876**   Prior to the final, successful struggle for independence (1810–21), Mexico had only two organized economic activities, agriculture (including livestock raising) and mining (chiefly gold and silver). Except for isolated pockets where the colonial officers governed and lived, there were neither internal improvements nor the most rudimentary amenities of organized life. For most Mexicans, living was a process of eking out subsistence.

The half-century that immediately followed independence has been characterized as "hectic" and "catastrophic," principally because it was a period of unrelieved political instability. Thirty different persons served as President, heading more than fifty different governments. In addition to domestic violence triggered by rebellions and *coups d'état*, the Mexicans fought two wars with the French (1838 and 1862–67) and one with the United States (1846–48). The half-century-plus, as a result, was one of virtual stagnation in the economy: the agricultural sector grew only slowly, output of the silver mines in 1875 was at the same level as in 1810, and only minimal internal improvements were made. The only notable economic achievement was the establishment of a textile industry, which enjoyed relative prosperity under the umbrella of high tariffs and other kinds of governmental protection.[4]

**The Porfirian period**   The Porfirian period—so called because one man, Porfirio Díaz, ruled Mexico for 31 of the 35 years between 1876 and 1911—was markedly different from the preceding one. It was characterized by slow but sustained growth.

> [While] population grew at an annual rate of 1.4 percent over the period, the corresponding rate for gross domestic product was approximately 2.7 percent, according to the best available estimate . . . the latter 35 years witnessed the spread of commercial agricultural production for both the domestic and foreign market, the gradual demise of the craftsman in the face of factory competition, growing export diversification, and the importation of producers' goods in ever-increasing proportions.[5]

Several factors converged to put Mexico on a growth path. Law and order, even if not justice, were firmly established by a strong central government. In Roger Hansen's words, "Opposition was placated or decapitated depending upon the circumstances."[6] Second, there was a huge inflow of American, British, and French investment, much of which was spent to build a railway system that greatly expanded the size of the domestic market and also facilitated Mexican sellers' access to foreign markets. Third, economic opportunities for indigenous entrepreneurs blossomed and were seized.

But the Porfirian era had a dark side, and that as much as anything else brought about its end. As so commonly happens during the development process, the rich got richer and the poor got poorer.[7] Specifically, the distribution of land ownership, already very unequal, became more so. In addition, although a high death rate held down the rate of population growth, job oppor-

[4] This section and the next draw heavily upon Roger D. Hansen, *Mexican Economic Development: The Roots of Rapid Growth*, Studies in Development Progress, No. 2 (Washington, D.C.: National Planning Association, 1971), Ch. II.

[5] Hansen, *op. cit.*, p. 12.

[6] *Ibid.*, p. 12.

[7] "For the longest part of the development process . . . the primary impact of economic development on income distribution is, on the average, to decrease both the absolute and the relative incomes of the poor." Irma Adelman, "Development Economics—A Reassessment of Goals," *American Economic Review*, May 1975, p. 302.

tunities grew even more slowly, causing unemployment to rise. Most distressingly, while output of raw materials from Mexico's farms rose dramatically, production of food and beverages *declined*. By the end of the Porfirian era, in short, an untold number of Mexicans were both landless and in grinding poverty. It was in their name primarily that the overthrow of Porfirio Díaz was organized and carried out.

**The post-revolutionary period**　As so often happens, the revolution was costly in life and property. For nearly ten years Mexico was torn by internal strife, compounded by American military intervention in 1914. Devastation was widespread; crop and livestock production fell sharply. Worst of all, more than one million Mexicans—more than 7 percent of the population—lost their lives as a result of the revolution.

By 1921, however, the paroxysm had ended, a considerable measure of political stability was reestablished, and economic development had been resumed. Between 1921 and 1926, for example, real national income rose 20 percent, despite continued stagnation in agriculture and petroleum extraction. Thereafter and until 1940, gross domestic product rose only modestly and GDP per capita actually fell, a result mainly of the adverse impact upon Mexico of the worldwide Great Depression.

It is clear in retrospect that the first three post-revolutionary decades, marked though they were by little improvement in Mexicans' well-being, were the years in which the foundation was laid for Mexico's subsequent economic surge. Fortified with a constitution that had general support and was carefully respected by political leaders, during the 1920s and 1930s Mexico came of age governmentally. During those years, too, the land-reform program was institutionalized and the power of the *hacendados* broken, a strong monetary and financial system was constructed, and a free labor market was created to provide gainful employment for those who left or were displaced from agriculture. As Morris Singer has put it, "Mexico was technically and institutionally pre-conditioned for sustained growth by 1940 and . . . merely awaited some favorable shock to move forward."[8]

**The rapid-growth period**　The "favorable shock" came in the

[8] Morris Singer, *op. cit.*, p. 19.

## TABLE 4-2

## Mexican Output and Population, by Year, 1952–75
### Indexes with 1952 = 100

| YEAR | AGRICULTURAL OUTPUT | INDUSTRIAL OUTPUT | TOTAL GROSS DOMESTIC PRODUCT | POPULATION |
|------|---------------------|-------------------|------------------------------|------------|
| 1952 | 100 | 100 | 100 | 100 |
| 1953 | 100 | 99  | 100 | 103 |
| 1954 | 118 | 107 | 111 | 106 |
| 1955 | 129 | 118 | 120 | 110 |
| 1956 | 125 | 131 | 129 | 113 |
| 1957 | 136 | 140 | 138 | 117 |
| 1958 | 145 | 147 | 146 | 121 |
| 1959 | 141 | 158 | 150 | 125 |
| 1960 | 148 | 171 | 162 | 129 |
| 1961 | 152 | 178 | 168 | 134 |
| 1962 | 161 | 187 | 177 | 138 |
| 1963 | 164 | 205 | 188 | 143 |
| 1964 | 174 | 232 | 207 | 148 |
| 1965 | 183 | 244 | 215 | 153 |
| 1966 | 186 | 272 | 230 | 159 |
| 1967 | 192 | 292 | 244 | 164 |
| 1968 | 198 | 321 | 264 | 170 |
| 1969 | 199 | 347 | 281 | 177 |
| 1970 | 209 | 376 | 301 | 182 |
| 1971 | 213 | 385 | 311 | 188 |
| 1972 | 215 | 421 | 333 | 195 |
| 1973 | 216 | 459 | 359 | 202 |
| 1974 | 221 | 484 | 381 | 209 |
| 1975 | 230 | 506 | 398 | 216 |

SOURCES: Output indexes derived from absolute estimates for 1952–64 in Clark W. Reynolds, *The Mexican Economy* (New Haven: Yale University Press, 1970), pp. 371–73, for 1965–73 in Banco de México, *Informe Anual 1973*, pp. 92–95, and for 1974–75 in Banco de Mexico, *Review of the Economic Situation of Mexico*, Sept. 1975, pp. 311–16 (1975 data are estimates).

The population index is derived from estimates in United Nations, *Demographic Yearbook 1970*, pp. 128–29, and United Nations, *Monthly Bulletin of Statistics*, Sept. 1975, p. 3, plus extension of the 1974 growth rate to 1975.

form of World War II. As a nonbelligerent safely removed from the arenas of devastation and with a sizable pool of unemployed and underemployed human and physical resources to draw upon, Mexico took full advantage of a war-induced spurt in demand for its exports. The exporting industries necessarily expanded in size, in the process stimulating domestic income and consumption. This in turn prompted the establishment of domestic enterprises for the production of substitutes for imported goods. Between 1940 and 1950, as a result, gross domestic product in real terms rose 91 percent; the value of manufacturing output, 86 percent; and the value of agricultural product, 74 percent (Table 4-1). In all but one of the wartime years, moreover, Banco de México added handsomely to its holdings of foreign exchange.

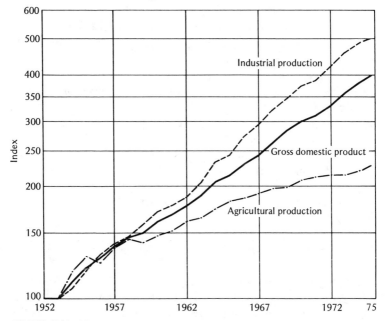

**FIG. 4-1**
**Estimated Output of the Mexican Economy,**
**by Year, 1952–75**

(Indexes with 1952 = 100, logarithmic vertical scale)

SOURCE: Table 4-2.

The impetus to economic growth provided by the war was effectively exploited in the ensuing three decades. For the 1940s as a whole, the average yearly rise in total real output was about 6.7 percent; for the 1950s, about 6 percent; for the 1960s, nearly 7 percent. Growth in real terms was achieved in all sectors but especially in industry; by the late 1960s Mexico was supplying most of its own consumption of basic petroleum products, steel, processed foodstuffs, and a variety of technically complex consumers' goods (such as automotive parts, color television sets, and air-conditioning units). And the stock of social overhead capital was vastly greater than in 1940, thanks to continually heavy expenditures on irrigation systems, the transportation network, and electric power facilities, among other things.

A number of factors conspired to produce these results. One was the availability, especially in the earlier years of the postwar period, of a large pool of unemployed and underemployed resources, human and physical, that could be and were shifted to more productive uses. Another was the presence of a group of private entrepreneurs who took advantage of the economic opportunities created by rising internal demand. Perhaps most important were the policies and practices of the Mexican government, which (a) guided its war-generated reserves of foreign exchange into capital goods imports; (b) promoted the expansion and diversification of domestic industry through a mixture of restrictions upon importation of consumers' goods and financial assistance—subsidies, loans, and direct investments; (c) financed much of its public-works expenditures from its own savings, principally, tax surpluses plus "profits" from state enterprises; (d) constructed a strong and sophisticated set of financial institutions, without which no modern economy can prosper; and (e) thanks in largest part to its ability during 1955–70 to achieve all this while restraining price inflation to an average yearly rise of roughly 3 percent, preserved political harmony and tranquility at home.

## ECONOMIC PERFORMANCE AND PROSPECTS

**Plenty**  In the nearly four decades that have elapsed since 1940, Mexico has moved rapidly in the direction of national affluence. Of this there are numerous indicators: marked growth in GDP per capita (an average annual rate of 3.3 percent during 1960–

73), despite an unusually high rate of population growth; dramatic enlargement in the number of consumers' goods that are domestically produced in whole or substantial part; lengthened life expectancy, together with marked improvement in the quantity and quality of medical and dental care; striking gains in the rate of functional literacy. Phrased more pungently, for many Mexicans, especially rural residents, "growth has meant beds instead of the ground, bread as well as tortillas, travel by bus as well as by burro, and doctors instead of *curanderos*. . . . The low income group has acquainted itself with beer, radios, and tableware; while the middle class has been exposed to such luxuries as gas stoves, electric blenders, whiskey, nylons, television, and automobiles (which they tend to drive in Mexico City in truly frantic and frenzied fashion)."[9] While Mexico in the mid-1970s was far from eligible for membership in the select group of rich economies, it had long since left the ranks of the world's poor countries.

It is tempting to project Mexico's recent economic performance into the future, forecasting that in a relatively few years it will achieve a condition of full-blown plenty. But extrapolation is a hazardous exercise, especially in a world characterized by swift changes in technology, relative prices, trade flows, and the like. Notably uncertain in Mexico's case is its ability in future to keep its agricultural growth rate ahead of its population growth rate. From 1952 through 1975, agricultural output grew at the rate of 3.7 percent annually while population was growing 3.4 percent per year. Sown area expanded, irrigation increased, and farming technology improved substantially. Much potential remains unrealized, but clearly the sooner Mexico can achieve a balanced structure of low death rates and low birth rates, the more assured its future will be.

**Economic justice and freedom**　Growth in total and per capita output has been accompanied by a modest improvement in the degree of equality of opportunity. We have already noted the growing percentage of Mexicans with several years of formal schooling and attending institutions of higher education. Similarly, a growing fraction of the population enjoys genuine freedom of choice among occupations and job locations; it is no longer the rule, scarcely excepted, that children must do the same kind of

[9] *Ibid.*, p. 37.

work in the same place as their parents. As a corollary, the figurative (and often literal) walls separating socioeconomic strata are no longer virtually impenetrable; rather they are developing more and larger pores through which "bottom dogs" (especially Indians) can progress and "top dogs" regress. On the order of 2,500,000 workers are unionized, and the millions more who are not are protected in law, if not always in fact, by a minimum-wage statute. The status of women, once lowly indeed in a society thoroughly dominated by males and their reverence for *machismo*, has changed perceptibly. In 1947 women won the right to vote and in 1953 the right to hold national as well as municipal elective office. Their labor force participation rate has climbed from less than 7 percent in 1930 to an estimated 20-plus percent in 1970; and though most working women are in occupations in the lower ranges of the job hierarchy, the number in well-paid, prestigious positions is on the increase.

Although these steps toward egalitarianism are noteworthy, they leave Mexico far short of the point where it could legitimately be described as equitable. Inequality is deeply embedded in the Mexican political economy. One indicator of this condition is the personal distribution of money income, shown in Table 4-3 for 1963 (the latest year for which data are available). The top 10 percent of the family population received about 42 percent of total income, whereas the bottom tenth received only 2 percent; and the share of the top 20 percent was 59 percent, compared with only 6 percent for the bottom fifth. Disparities of a similar magnitude characterize the pattern of land ownership, despite the lengthy and extensive land-redistribution program. More than three-fourths of all private land owners control roughly a tenth of private cropland, whereas in some Mexican states over 90 percent of private croplands are held by under 2 percent of the private landowners.

There are many reasons for believing, and only a few for disbelieving, that the economic freedoms lately won by several million Mexicans will soon be enjoyed by most or all others in the population. Only some unforeseen catastrophe that utterly disrupted the political and economic framework, such as runaway inflation or prolonged depression, would return Mexico to a condition in which there was very little or no freedom of occupational choice, limited geographical mobility, limited access to educational opportunities, and economic subjugation of ethnic minorities and

## TABLE 4-3
## Personal Income Distribution in Mexico, 1963
### (Percentages, by deciles of families)

| DECILES | | PERCENTAGE OF TOTAL INCOME | CUMULATIVE INCOME |
|---|---|---|---|
| I | | 2.0 | 2.0 |
| II | | 2.0 | 4.0 |
| III | | 2.5 | 6.5 |
| IV | | 4.5 | 11.0 |
| V | | 4.5 | 15.5 |
| VI | | 6.0 | 21.5 |
| VII | | 8.0 | 29.5 |
| VIII | | 11.5 | 41.0 |
| IX | | 17.5 | 58.5 |
| X | 5.0 | 14.5 | 73.0 |
| | 2.5 | 11.0 | 84.0 |
| | 2.5 | 16.0 | 100.0 |
| Total | | 100.0 | |

SOURCE: Roger D. Hansen, *Mexican Economic Development: The Roots of Rapid Growth* (Washington, D.C.: National Planning Association, Studies in Development Progress, No. 2, 1971), Table IV-1, p. 73.

women. In these and correlative aspects of Mexican life, egalitarianism seems to be a firmly established norm.

The prospects for significantly reducing inequities in income and wealth, however, are uncertain as long as Mexico's political economy continues to include a trio of institutions—the market economy, private property ownership, and democratic policy-making procedures. The first two all but guarantee unequal rewards and unequal accumulations. Efforts to offset these inequalities, whether through progressive taxation, subsidies in cash or kind to those at the low end of the distribution, or redistributive expenditures, can be held in check by "haves" who are both determined to preserve their favored position and skilled in influencing the processes of democratic decision-making. Those, in short, who benefit from the market system and private property ownership can and usually do defend their privileges successfully through control of the political process. Consequently, only an upheaval comparable to that which began in Cuba in 1959 is

*Poor Man's Burden*

likely to produce in Mexico a major redistribution of wealth and income.[10] Whether the resulting socioeconomic benefits would be greater or less than the socioeconomic costs of upheaval is, of course, a serious moral and political issue.

**Stability and security**    In highly industrialized economies, the chief problem confronting economic stabilizers is how to minimize unemployment and underemployment while holding general price rises to a "reasonable" rate. Because rates of unemployment and underemployment tend to vary inversely with the rate of inflation, stabilization policy in mature economies commonly has a "stop–go" character. As soon as policies to raise the employment rate yield the desired result, they must be reversed in order to restrain a rising rate of inflation. In Mexico, by contrast, relatively high

[10] Compare Irma Adelman, *op. cit.*, p. 303: "The price of economic equity is high: a necessary condition for its achievement is radical structural change."

rates of joblessness and "disguised" unemployment are chronic and indicate economic immaturity rather than economic instability. The chief problem for stabilization policy is how to restrain price inflation without unduly restricting the rate of output growth.

Compared to other developing nations in Latin America, Africa, and Asia, Mexico's past record of achievement in managing the trade-off has been very respectable, even if not outstanding. From 1940 to 1954 the emphasis was upon output growth at the pain of an average annual increase of 10 percent in the general price level. By the end of the period, real incomes of all but entrepreneurs had eroded so severely that

> "protests among the middle- and lower-income classes occurred throughout the country, and private sector confidence in the government's development policies seemed broken. At no other time since the PRI [Mexico's governing party] assumed command of the Mexican presidency and politics had criticism of the present system of government been so harsh and outspoken."[11]

Since 1955, understandably, price stabilization has taken precedence over growth, although the latter has not been sacrificed to obtain the former. Through skillful use of monetary and financial policies, for 15 years the rate of inflation was held to an average of 3 percent per year while national output grew on the order of 6 percent annually. Not until the early 1970s did rapid inflation reappear, and that was a result mainly of events over which Mexico had little control and which similarly affected all nations, rich and poor and in-between.

Can Mexico repeat in future its past success in achieving substantial growth in output with only a moderate inflation rate? In its favor are such assets as its experienced corps of policy-makers and its sophisticated institutional framework. But the policy-makers and the institutions will have to cope with new kinds of challenge, two in particular. First, as a decidedly "open" economy in that it depends heavily upon trade with the rest of the world, Mexico cannot immunize itself against the dramatic changes now occurring and likely to recur in the world raw materials market—in the supply of and demand for petroleum, sugar, fertilizers, metals, and the like. Second, as the Mexican

[11] Roger D. Hansen, *op. cit.*, p. 49.

economy progresses toward maturity, its policy-makers will have to pay more and more attention to the achievement of domestic full employment and consequently to the management of the conflict between that objective and the goal of price stability.

**Growth**    Addressing what he labeled the dilemma of Mexico's development, the American economist Raymond Vernon concluded in 1963 that the country's future growth rate would be much slower than it had been in the preceding quarter-century. As he saw it, Mexico no longer had a "leading sector," a major stimulant, to rapid economic growth. Exportation of farm products and minerals, the main engine of growth in the previous twenty years, was no longer vigorous; import substitution was so far advanced that it could not qualify as successor to the "lead role"; the small size of the domestic market seriously inhibited private expenditures for widening and deepening the capital stock; and public investment would have to be restricted by the government's inability to finance the necessary outlays through taxation or borrowing. He concluded that stagnation was the Mexican economy's future character.[12]

In most respects, this gloomy forecast proved inaccurate, even in the half-dozen years after it was offered. Traditional exports did grow only slowly. But other export goods entered world markets in growing number and volume, tourism expanded markedly, private investment mounted in both existing and new industries, and public revenues grew considerably faster than gross national product. And by the time Vernon's prediction was ten years old, even his pessimism about traditional exports had been overtaken by events. High and rising demand for agricultural products and petroleum in world markets put Mexico in a position at least to be largely self-sufficient in these areas, at best to enjoy high export prices.

To all its other growth-promoting assets must be added Mexico's enviable position in international politics. On its northern boundary lies the United States, with which Mexico has had peaceful, if not friendly, relations for the last 60 years. On or near its southern frontier are small Central American states, none of which presents a threat to Mexico's national security. Its mili-

[12] Raymond Vernon, *The Dilemma of Mexico's Development* (Cambridge, Mass.: Harvard University Press, 1963).

tary establishment, as a result, is of very modest size—which is to say that, unlike India and China, Mexico sees no need to divert resources from economic growth into a burdensome army, navy, and air force.

Only a dogmatic optimist would insist, given the great uncertainties that characterize the 1970s, that Mexico's drive to economic maturity will proceed rapidly and without serious interruption. That seems, however, to be a much better guess than not.

## SUGGESTED READINGS

Morris Singer, *Growth, Equality, and the Mexican Experience* (Austin, Texas and London: Published by the University of Texas Press for the Institute of Latin American Studies, 1969).

> Extensive investigation of the impact of economic development upon the distribution of income and wealth in Mexico.

Roger D. Hansen, *Mexican Economic Development: The Roots of Rapid Growth* (Washington, D.C.: National Planning Association, 1971).

> A concise summary of Mexico's recent economic history.

Clark W. Reynolds, *The Mexican Economy: Twentieth Century Structure and Growth* (New Haven and London: Yale University Press, 1970).

> A broad analysis of Mexico's experience in economic development.

# THE SOVIET UNION

5

The USSR has a mainly collectivist economy, only now approaching maturity. After harsh beginnings, it has grown rapidly and steadily for the last quarter century, pushing some forms of output to very impressive levels while leaving others in shocking backwardness. What accounts for this pattern of unequal achievements?

The institutions of the Soviet economy have a deceptive familiarity: money and prices, wages and salaries, stores and factories, taxes and pensions. Yet the motive forces in the economy are different from those in the United States. What makes the system work?

The Soviet record of economic growth has genuinely impressive features that stand out even after exaggerations and distortions of the Stalin era have been removed. Which parts of the economy have grown? When? How fast? What are the prospects for future growth?

These questions are discussed in this chapter. In addition, we review the performance of the Soviet economy in terms of the criteria laid down in Chapter 1. In three of the five areas of performance the Soviet record is good; but are the benefits worth their costs?

## A COMMAND ECONOMY

A command economy, more than others, must decide on goals and organize itself to pursue them. The Soviet economy, for almost fifty years, has been tightly organized in pursuit of well-defined goals that deserve our close attention. Many of its economic institutions resemble those of a market economy, yet they are distinctively employed to produce results markedly different from those achieved by the U.S. economy. We should examine the organization of these institutions before we turn to the record of Soviet growth and weigh the performance of the system.

**Party controls and the structure of the economy**    The Soviet economy is a command economy, controlling most resource use through direct orders rather than relative prices. The Communist Party of the Soviet Union establishes basic national policy objectives, which in turn imply major economic goals and lead to production targets. In driving toward these targets the party uses both physical allocation orders and a price mechanism resembling that of a market economy. The results are mainly shaped, however, by centralized authority and not by decentralized consumer desires.

At the center of the economy stands a vast State sector, made up of state-owned factories, mines, railroads, construction firms, stores, and other producing units. This sector deals with some 60 million Soviet households, about equally divided between town and country. From urban households it obtains services paid for in salaries or wages, and to them it sells consumer goods. From rural households it obtains agricultural produce paid for in various ways, and to them it sells consumer goods, though rural households do not fare as well as urban households in their dealings with the State. Urban households buy a good deal of their food from rural households for cash, in collective-farm markets at free-market prices. The State sector produces, along with consumer goods, a massive flow of capital plant and equipment, military items, and a variety of governmental services such as education and medical care.

**Soviet economic institutions**    A Soviet factory or other State enterprise is generally supposed to cover its costs and make a profit. Its initial capital comes from the State. Much of its profits will be taxed into the central budget, and most of its expansion capital will come by grant from the central budget. In current operations it is under pressure to keep costs below revenue, although high-priority items will be liberally subsidized. The Soviet enterprise is not unlike a subsidiary unit in a great American corporation, with the enterprise acting the part of a Chevrolet plant, for example, and the State in the role of General Motors.

A Soviet urban household will typically contain several income earners. Before the early 1960s, the real wage of a single breadwinner would not support his family. Thus, family members—perhaps including retired workers getting pensions—pool their incomes, while each is to some extent self-supporting. And Soviet urban households, by world standards, are small; the 1970 census showed only 18 percent of urban families with more than four members.

Fourteen million peasant households reside in 30,000 *kolkhozy*, or collective farms, which account for 46 percent of the country's sown area. A large part of the *kolkhoz's* output goes to the State. The remainder, together with some of the proceeds from cash sales to the State, is divided among *kolkhoz* members in proportion to the number of workdays each has contributed during the year. The *kolkhoz* typically contains around 450 peasant households, with from 2,000 to 12,000 or more acres under crops. About half the total cropland is operated by 17,300 *sovkhozy*, or State farms, which employ on the average over 600 workers (on a wage basis) and average 20,000 acres of cropland. The remaining 3 percent of Soviet cropland is intensively farmed in small private plots by peasants and urban workers; this small residual area nevertheless continues to account for 20 percent of all agricultural output.

Outside the State sector some two million individuals provide services to the public. Doctors, dentists, and lawyers have a few private clients; clothes, shoes, watches, and household utensils are repaired; and myriad articles are sold or resold in shops, stalls, or market squares—with the grudging approval of the authorities. These people operate as individuals or in small cooperative groups called *artels*, but they are not allowed to hire anyone else's labor.

Transactions between the State and the public, both workers and peasants, and within the State sector itself are centrally managed. Though transactions between workers and peasants are not controlled, the State, as we shall see, can intervene here too.

**Money flows, taxes, and incomes**   In a command economy the government need not pay for the resources it uses; consequently —one would think—it need not collect tax revenue from the people. Yet taxes play a vital role in the USSR. Money flows out from the State to the public when wages and salaries are paid and comes back to the State sector when consumer goods are bought, except when it passes from urban workers into peasant mattresses. But the wage and salary income far exceeds the value of consumer goods available. The excess must somehow be siphoned off; otherwise, too much pressure would be put on the prices of consumer goods.

The government could tax consumer goods directly, tax the revenues of producing enterprises, or tax the income of wage and salary earners. In the USSR, chief reliance has been placed on very large excise ("turnover") taxes, especially on items like bread, to siphon mass purchasing power into the State treasury. The turnover tax has at times constituted almost two-thirds of the retail value of consumer goods. Recently its relative contribution to State revenues has declined, while taxes laid directly on producing enterprises have been increasingly relied upon. Still, the difference between aggregate wage earnings and the labor cost of consumer goods is effectively channeled through the State treasury.

One important money flow runs outside this two-way channel between the public and the State: consumer food purchases in collective farm markets. Here, wage income is used to buy what the peasants grow in their private truck gardens, along with any excess produce from collective farms. In bad times, prices in collective farm markets rise manyfold. Peasants will spend as little time as possible in collective farm work and shift to their private plots. At the end of World War II, billions of rubles had thus accumulated in peasant hands.

This purchasing power, hanging over the consumer goods market, was neatly confiscated by the government in December 1947, when old rubles were called in and new ones issued, one for ten. Wages, however, were immediately paid in the new rubles, and small bank balances were exchanged one for one. Workers generally had small savings accounts, while peasants held their savings in cash. The "reform" thus discriminated harshly against the peasants. By contrast the 1961 exchange of one new ruble for ten old ones was accompanied by a tenfold reduction in all prices and wages. The effect was to make economic numbers more convenient while leaving everyone's relative position unchanged.

**Soviet economic planning**   Within this institutional framework the party leadership has developed a distinctive kind of economic planning, conditioned both by its aims and by the political setting of the USSR. Since 1928, economic plans have been designed to raise the output of high-priority commodities as rapidly as possible. In focusing efforts on these commodities the regime has used the full range of pressures open to a totalitarian system. Thus, the aim has not been placid balance, and the means have not had to wait on popular consent.

Soviet planning stresses the development of heavy industry. Each year in late spring the Presidium of the Party's Central Committee issues a handful of overall targets for steel output, electric power production, machinery production, and so on, for the coming year. During the summer, Gosplan (the Soviet central planning board) translates these major control figures into several hundred required commodity production goals. These go out to regional or sectoral production authorities, who subdivide them among individual factories. Lists of the inputs needed to meet the individual targets are then assembled and passed up the line to Moscow. During the fall, Gosplan seeks to balance what may now be some 1500 interconnected production targets where in general the demands of industrial users are likely to exceed the supplies being set up. Finally, by the year's end, after negotiation and adjustment, a more or less consistent set of targets is confirmed by party and government as next year's annual plan.

The central variables here are not prices, but input supplies, output targets, and the rate at which technological improvements can be brought into operation. Plan administrators seek to push and pull everyone along as rapidly as possible. The production targets of successive annual plans act like a constantly receding horizon, forever calling the traveler forward. Industrial enterprises live within a chronic atmosphere of shortages, mild for high-priority activities and crippling for activities at the outer edge of the government's concern.

These plans are always tight. Cutting back the demands for one product, say coal, to the level of anticipated availabilities may endanger the production of another product, say steel, that is needed for coal-producing equipment and therefore contributes to achieving the coal target. Yet strictness in doling out inputs may induce both coal and steel producers to improve their efficiency by lowering input use per unit of output. Flexibility within tight plans is obtained through placing some current supplies at the disposal of the central authorities. When crises develop, these reserves can be sent to high-priority users. At the end of the year, those targets in which the authorities are interested will be fulfilled, with low-priority items bearing the impact of any shortages.

Key industrial inputs are distributed among claimants through physical allocation orders, much as the War Production Board allocated steel in the United States during World War II. State prices are conventionally low, so that high prices (reflecting relative scarcities) are not allowed to ration supplies toward their most-wanted applications. In practice, various quasi-prices or trade-off ratios are recognized by plant managers and influence their day-to-day decisions, although such ratios lack official standing. The planning authorities allocate resources, not in response to price signals, but by administrative fiat reflecting current party priorities. In this way, party preferences intercept and replace the consumer preferences that determine resource allocation in a market economy.

**Operating problems in Soviet planning** Soviet experience shows that this kind of planning can raise the output of selected products rapidly. The Soviet economy has neither ground to a halt nor collapsed in chaos. The record also shows, however, that various operating difficulties arise, impairing the efficiency of the system. Important among these are the problems of "success indicators" and resistance to innovation.

The managers of Soviet factories—and of all other units subject to the plan—always find themselves confronted with several targets to meet, which usually are quantitative and broad. One reason is that few producing units turn out only a single product; many produce hundreds of different items. The plan cannot specify all the targets individually and will therefore call for "500,000 tons of fabricated steel" or "100,000 rubles worth of cotton knit goods." In seeking to reach difficult aggregate targets, however, plant officials are likely to choose the easiest component mixture open to them. Consider, for example, the nail producer: If he is told to produce so many tons of nails, he will produce more large ones and fewer small ones than the planners want. If the nail target is given in value terms, he will specialize in turning out fancy, high-value nails. If the nail target is given in numbers of nails, the producer will turn out tiny ones.

When success is measured in terms of quantitative targets, whether single or multiple, quality suffers. Soviet plan administrators have found it necessary to police those who skimp on product quality to meet production goals. And since these quantitative targets are difficult to attain, the system is plagued with reports that are juggled so that success can be achieved at least on paper. Defective production can be passed off as acceptable; a little of next month's production can be credited to this month's target; or perhaps the mixture of items produced can be adjusted toward those easiest to make, whether or not they are the most desired.

Hard-pressed plant managers also respond to ambitious production targets by showing a marked resistance to the installation of new machines or new methods, as this interrupts production. In recent years the regime has laid special stress on technological innovation and has run into serious passive resistance from factory officials. Plan-fulfillment bonuses are now tied to the installation of new methods so that factory managers will cooperate with modernization even when it cuts into the current month's output.

The resistance shown by plant managers toward equipment and process innovations also appears among the plan authorities themselves. Annual increases can most easily be planned along familiar lines: more steel, more lathes, or more timber. Major campaigns have been necessary to shift investment and production plans toward plastics, petrochemicals, electronics, and similar new areas that have shown promise in the West.

**Commanding with signals**   In recent years, it has become clear to both Soviet and Western observers that the crude methods of Stalinist planning cannot deal effectively with the current problems of the Soviet economy. Where once there were a dozen producers of a particular product, there may now be scores. Key products used to number a few hundred; now there are thousands of them. The surge of technological innovations that has swept over Western economies in the last quarter century offers a bewildering variety of choices to Soviet industrial planners. Coordination of tens of thousands of inputs and outputs, moving among thousands of factories scattered in hundreds of Soviet towns and cities, has placed increasing strain on plan administration.

In the search for consistency and efficiency, Soviet technicians have turned for guidance to the concepts of input–output and linear programming. The basic notions of linear programming (a mathematical way of finding an optimum subject to linear constraints), were laid down by L. V. Kantorovich at the University of Leningrad in 1939, but little attention was paid to his work until the late 1950s. Under the sponsorship of the late V. S. Nemchinov, a whole school of mathematical economists has come into being. Large-scale efforts are under way to formulate national production plans in input–output terms and to find optimal solutions to plant-size production and investment problems through linear and nonlinear programming.

Since the principles that underlie efficient and optimal resource use are the same for all economies, no matter who owns the means of production, Soviet economists have increasingly been led to analyze their allocation and investment problems along familiar Western lines. When resources are being applied with optimal efficiency, their relative values take the form of an equilibrium set of relative prices. These are the prices that would theoretically be reached in the long run under pure competition. Theoretically they could be computed and issued by Gosplan to serve as a set of signals that would guide all producing and consuming units toward correct decisions without any physical commands. Thus, within the State sector, individual producing units making decentralized decisions might be led voluntarily to follow party intentions. Here "optimum" and "efficient" would be defined in relation to the desires of the Communist Party. No such sophisticated procedure is yet established in the USSR, but tentative moves in this direction are already visible.

A second powerful force for change is now exerted by Soviet consumers, who are no longer in such desperate need of clothing, household wares, and other consumer goods that they willingly buy whatever reaches the stores. Unfashionable clothing, poorly made shoes, and defective sewing machines now go unsold. Since this clearly wastes resources even though quantitative output targets are being met, the authorities have called for experiments in which producers will adjust the quality and quantity of their output to what consumers want. Production of undesired items will be curtailed. On the other hand, it is by no means assured that production of items in great demand will be increased without limit. For one thing, the party may have higher priority uses for the inputs that go into these products.

More fundamentally, the Soviet vision of "full Communism," as spelled out in the revised Party program of 1961, calls for an abundance of goods and services to meet the "rational" needs of a "cultured" person. Senseless proliferation of consumer durables in individual households is less "rational" than, for example, a row of washing machines in the basement of an apartment house, at least in official eyes. And other consumer goods, like comic books, are clearly not "cultured." The planners are therefore likely to supervise producers' responses to consumers' demands, holding back on items deemed unsuitable by the authorities. The sovereignty of the Soviet consumer will be far from unlimited.

## THE SOVIET GROWTH MECHANISM

The economic power of the Soviet state has grown rapidly to massive dimensions. For almost fifty years, heavy burdens have been laid on the Russian people. Under Stalin's grim leadership, new methods for building national strength were devised. Under Khrushchev, the growth mechanism was loosened to produce all-around progress for a while. Since 1958 Soviet growth has slowed down, and the present leadership is casting about for ways to revive rapid progress. We shall review this whole record briefly and then examine Russia's potential for future growth.

**The historical background**  Although Russian modernization began with Peter the Great around 1700, it was only after 1861, when the serfs were liberated, that the process began to gather force. The Tsarist government intermittently spurred the change, relying to a large extent on individualist rather than collectivist institutions, especially after 1906. From the 1880s to 1913, industrial production grew at about 5 percent per year. In 1913 Russian steel production reached 4.5 million short tons, signaling the arrival of Russia as an industrial power.

But seven years of war and revolution wrecked the institutions that had produced this progress and severely damaged the economy. Not until 1928 was the USSR ready for further growth. From 1928 to 1940 the Soviet economy was driven forward along a twisted path toward industrial and military power. The power created was sufficient to withstand the Nazi invasion, but at the cost of great human tragedy and substantial damage to the economy. The World War II setback was made up by 1950. During the next decade, yearly additions to output reached large absolute size, with heavy industry, military power, and private consumption all growing simultaneously. What was the secret of this success?

**Stalin's development levers**    In the late 1920s the Stalinists discovered the levers that would move the whole economy rapidly, and regardless of popular wishes, toward industrial maturity. During the 1930s, during World War II, and during Stalin's postwar campaign (checked only by his death in 1953), these levers, in the unyielding grip of the party, regulated the Soviet growth mechanism. One basic lever controlled the terms of trade between agriculture and the State. The collective farm was organized as a collection center where the regime could lay hands on farm output, giving very little in return. Another lever controlled the real wages of the nonagricultural labor force; as consumer goods prices rose far above money wages in the 1930s, real wages were driven down sharply. The effect was to extract greatly increased labor input from the population, while deferring consumption rewards to the future. A third lever controlled the use of the social overhead capital (housing, municipal facilities, and the railroad system) that was inherited from Tsarist economic development; highly intensive use of this capital stock permitted investment to be concentrated in heavy industry.

Ample material was available for building the new system. The nonagricultural labor force grew from 15 to 35 million between 1928 and 1939. Rich natural resource deposits were vigorously exploited. The accumulated technological know-how of the West was freely drawn on: German, British, and American technicians; blueprints; equipment; and even complete factories were imported. Thus, the nonagricultural part of the economy could be rapidly built up.

**Collectivization and after**    The precondition for Stalinist industrial growth was, paradoxically, control over the agricultural sector that still dominated the economy in the 1920s. In 1916 and 1917, even before Lenin's revolution, the peasants had seized control of the land and its produce. They were willing to sell this produce if the prices they received were attractive in relation to prices of consumer goods. But the new regime wanted to build factories, not "waste" output on peasant consumption. Unless the peasants could be made to yield up a large fraction of each crop, the growth of heavy industry—in the absence of aid from abroad—would be slow. Consequently, Stalin launched a "second revolution" in the fall of 1929. Patience and persuasion gave way to violence. The reaction, too, was violent: rebellious peasants slaughtered half their livestock. By 1933, however, control over crop use was firmly in governmental hands. The output of a *kolkhoz* went first to the State; only after this demand had been met could the balance be divided among *kolkhoz* members. For twenty years thereafter, the agricultural sector was milked to provide the wherewithal for building heavy industry. Morale, labor productivity, and yield per acre were all very low, but industry and the armed forces were supplied with their needs.

From 1928 to 1953, Soviet net agricultural output rose only by 30 percent (including production on acquired territory), and since the population grew by 25 percent, the per capita gain was negligible. Stalin's system could exploit agriculture but could not improve it. His successors put through several institutional reforms that raised morale, productivity, and output very substantially without much investment. By 1958, output had increased some 50 percent over 1953; since then, in spite of massive State investment in agriculture, output growth has been modest. Bad weather causes a setback every few years (see Figure 5-1), and morale is still poor. Evidently, further basic remedies will be required if agriculture is to prosper. The lesson to be drawn from the period as a whole is clear: modern, efficient agriculture is not attained by Soviet means. Low-income nations had best look elsewhere for a model of agricultural reform.

**Soviet investment in growth**     State control over agriculture and urban wages gave the Soviet regime the power to shift resources from consumption into capital formation. But it has mainly been the distinctive manner of using these resources that explains the rapid growth of Soviet industrial and military power. The process is one of "investment in investment," leading to what Professor Lloyd Reynolds of Yale wryly calls an "input–input system." When steel is produced, it goes heavily into mining machinery, freight cars, or rolling mill equipment, so that more steel can be produced—for still further plowing back into still more industrial growth. Results do not appear overnight, but after two or three decades the (compounded) effect becomes very large indeed.

Some forms of capital formation lead to greater increases in output than other forms, and Soviet emphasis on lines of expansion with low capital–output ratios has speeded Soviet growth. Both the existing stock of capital plant and equipment and addi-

**FIG. 5-1**

**Indexes for Gross National Product, Industrial Production, and Agricultural Production, USSR, by Year, 1952–1974**

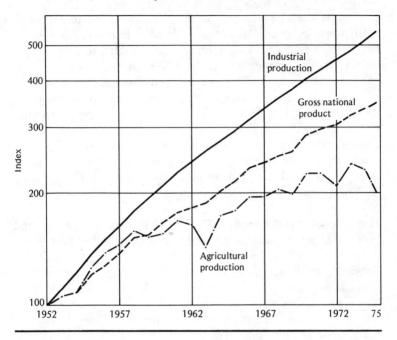

tions to it have been intensively used; this intensive use makes for lower capital–output ratios than would exist with relaxed use of capacity.

A related explanation for rapid short-run Soviet industrial growth concerns the treatment of depreciation and obsolescence. Cautious Western engineering and financial practice frequently leads to light utilization and prompt retirement of capital equipment. Competition may displace a piece of capital equipment long before its physical usefulness is over. In the USSR, however, the pressure of capital scarcity relative to Soviet objectives has led to a view that old equipment should be repaired, not retired. Until recently it was asserted that obsolescence is a capitalist myth. Clearly, a stubborn retention policy tends to raise current production costs, compared with what they would be with improved new equipment, and also tends toward a slower rate of technological progress than would emerge from prompt use of the latest advances. Nevertheless, it has proved to be a way of promoting maximum short-run *net* investment, since very little gross investment is offset by retirements.

In two sectors especially, Soviet practice has led to extraordinarily low average capital–output ratios. Urban housing and inter-city transportation typically require relatively high investment per unit of annual output, but in the USSR these facilities became unusally "productive." When apartments are filled with one or more families per room, the capital–output ratio for urban housing can be very low. Similarly, when freight trains run fairly continuously, night and day, seven days a week, regardless of the convenience of shippers and receivers, the roadway and rolling stock of a railroad system can be made to yield a very large annual flow of services. In both these respects, Soviet practice has gone far beyond any previous Western experience.

**The role of foreign trade**   During its first forty years, mutual hostility between the USSR and the outside world almost eliminated the kind of amiable foreign investment that had aided Russian growth before World War I. Soviet policy from 1917 through the middle 1950s stressed self-sufficiency, while Western buyers and sellers were nervous about trading with a Soviet government that conducted all its international business through a State monopoly, Amtorg. There was a brief spurt in Soviet imports and exports during the 1929–33 period and a large flow of wartime assistance to the USSR from her Western allies during 1942–1945. Normally, however, the Soviets' desire for economic independence prevented foreign aid or trade from playing much of a role in Soviet growth. It is quite true that the USSR imported many prototype models in establishing new lines of production. These prototypes embodied Western technology and were the indispensable carriers of progress. Such imports, however, were one-shot affairs and did not lead to a large, sustained volume of foreign trade.

After Stalin's death in 1953, Soviet foreign trade expanded greatly, most of it with other members of the Soviet bloc. Soviet trade with developing nations has grown even more rapidly, and for a few (Afghanistan, Cuba, Egypt, India, and Iraq, for example), trade with the USSR has become very important. But exchanges with the Soviet Union are still only a tiny fraction of the total trade of developing countries.

More recently, the USSR launched a determined campaign to import a new generation of industrial plant and equipment embodying the latest Western technology. Imports from Western Europe and Japan have grown markedly and the previously very small volume of trade with the United States has risen dramatically. While the full list of Soviet imports and exports is long and diverse, the major import categories cover industrial plant (such as heavy chemicals and synthetics) and advanced equipment (computers, pipeline compressors, electronic components, and so forth). In addition, there is now a substantial volume of feedgrain imports to bolster the Soviet livestock sector. Soviet export earnings continue to come largely from the sale of minerals, timber, and unsophisticated manufactures. The recent sharp increases in the prices of gold and crude oil have also greatly enlarged the USSR's foreign-exchange receipts.

**Influences on prospective Soviet growth**   Where growth is concerned, the factors of production should be reviewed in this order: technology, entrepreneurship, capital, labor, and land. Technological progress and improved organization are the main contributors to growth; additions to capital come next; more (or better) labor follows; land (or, more broadly, resources) is now seen as material to be exploited by modern scientists. In this perspective, what are the prospects for Soviet economic growth?

Before World War II the USSR selected from advanced Western technology the industrial processes and products that appeared essential for building a strong industrial base. After wartime destruction and recovery, duplication and extension of this base required very little additional innovation. Meanwhile, the marked advances in Western technology that have developed since 1940 have not been promptly utilized outside the defense-related sectors of the Soviet economy. There thus remains much unrealized potential for further Soviet output expansion as advanced technology spreads to all sectors of the economy. The last few years have shown, however, that technological transfer is by no means easy in the face of bureaucratic resistance and institutional barriers. Soviet catching up is likely to be gradual in this area, and the USSR's capacity to produce important innovations on its own has yet to be demonstrated.

Though the Soviet stock of fixed capital plant and equipment has continued to grow steadily, its effectiveness has diminished. Lavish investments in agriculture have shown disappointing results. Massive industrial capital increments have been slow in reaching full capacity and unimpressive in efficiency of performance. Large Soviet military and space programs have continued to pull a number of key industrial inputs away from the civilian economy. Investment in housing has absorbed a large volume of resources, but apartment building has slowed down despite remaining unmet needs. Now that the authorities are channeling more resources into passenger automobiles and other consumer durables, heavy industry's share of investment and therefore its further growth are harder to maintain.

Growth of the labor force, another major factor in past expansion of Soviet output, will not continue at its previous rate. Labor can no longer be pulled out of the agricultural sector without lowering farm output significantly, nor does any significant number of women remain outside the labor force. The average work week outside agriculture was reduced from 48 to 41 hours during the late 1950s, causing some of the decline in industrial output growth; if promises of a still shorter work week were to be put into effect, output growth might suffer further. The number of young men and women entering the labor force each year will level off and decline soon, reflecting low birth rates (except in Soviet Central Asia and the Caucasus). On the other hand, ample resources devoted to technical and scientific education continue to improve the quality of Soviet labor.

As can be seen in Figure 5-1 and Table 5-1, Soviet industrial production has grown at gradually declining rates over the last 25 years, while Soviet agricultural production has expanded erratically and to a far smaller extent. The growth rate for Soviet GNP as a whole has fallen from around 7 percent yearly in the 1950s to under 5 percent in the 1970s. Even if the agricultural sector shows healthy progress in the next few years, it seems highly unlikely that Soviet national income can grow again at a sustained 7 percent annual rate. The outlook is for perhaps a 4 to 5 percent annual increase in real Soviet GNP, permitting a rise in output per capita of at least 3 percent per year.

## TABLE 5-1

### Indexes for Agricultural Output, Industrial Output, Gross National Product, and Population, USSR, by Year, 1952–75 (1952 = 100)

| YEAR | AGRICULTURAL OUTPUT | INDUSTRIAL OUTPUT | GROSS NATIONAL PRODUCT | POPULATION |
|------|------|------|------|------|
| 1952 | 100 | 100 | 100 | 100 |
| 1953 | 105 | 110 | 105 | 102 |
| 1954 | 108 | 123 | 110 | 103 |
| 1955 | 125 | 137 | 122 | 105 |
| 1956 | 139 | 151 | 129 | 107 |
| 1957 | 145 | 163 | 136 | 109 |
| 1958 | 157 | 179 | 151 | 111 |
| 1959 | 154 | 194 | 159 | 113 |
| 1960 | 155 | 210 | 166 | 115 |
| 1961 | 168 | 225 | 177 | 117 |
| 1962 | 164 | 242 | 183 | 119 |
| 1963 | 143 | 258 | 188 | 121 |
| 1964 | 173 | 274 | 203 | 123 |
| 1965 | 179 | 293 | 215 | 124 |
| 1966 | 195 | 313 | 229 | 126 |
| 1967 | 195 | 337 | 240 | 127 |
| 1968 | 205 | 358 | 251 | 128 |
| 1969 | 196 | 379 | 256 | 130 |
| 1970 | 225 | 407 | 283 | 131 |
| 1971 | 225 | 432 | 295 | 132 |
| 1972 | 209 | 454 | 302 | 133 |
| 1973 | 240 | 481 | 326 | 135 |
| 1974 | 232 | 514 | 336 | 136 |
| 1975 | 202 | 553 | 352 | 137 |

SOURCES: The Diamond-Krueger agricultural index and Greenslade-Robinson industrial index are from U.S. Congress, Joint Economic Committee, *Soviet Economic Prospects for the Seventies* (1973), pp. 335 and 220. The Cohn GNP estimates for 1955 and 1958–69 are from U.S. Congress, Joint Economic Committee, *Economic Performance . . .* (1970), p. 17. 1952–54 and 1956–57 GNP estimates are from Wilcox et al., *Economies of the World Today*, 2nd ed., p. 167. Population figures are from TsSU, *Narkhoz '67*, p. 7, and *Narkhoz '73*, p. 7. Output estimates for recent years are from unclassified releases issued by the Office of Economic Research, CIA.

## THE PERFORMANCE OF THE ECONOMY

In judging the Soviet economy by the several standards set forth in Chapter 1, we should recognize that the USSR now produces plenty, although its stress is on industrial and military power, not on consumer frivolities. And although national purposes constrain the alternatives, the Soviet people have substantial scope in their choice of goods, jobs, and place of residence. Equality of opportunity, upward mobility, and a relatively modest degree of income inequality combine to provide an impressive degree of equity. The system offers economic security too, in part by keeping demand ahead of supply. As to growth, steady industrial expansion has been accompanied by shaky agricultural gains, and serious gaps in the general welfare remain to be filled.

**Economic plenty**  The Soviet people are now serviceably supplied with food, shelter, and clothing. Public health services and competent medical care reach everyone. Most children complete seven years of education (no tuition charges), and many receive far more. Along with these fundamentals, sustained Soviet efforts have built the second most powerful state in the world: a state with massive nuclear, naval, and conventional ground forces; a vast flow of heavy industrial production; and more railroad freight traffic than anywhere else in the world. But these areas of weighty achievement are matched by other areas of very slow progress. Running water and indoor plumbing have yet to reach the last third of the population; unpaved roads still hamper movement for about half the population; and consumer services are skimpily supplied for almost everybody.

Soviet living standards differ from those of the United States not only in being markedly lower, but also in having a very different pattern. The way of life of the Russian people is quite different from the contemporary American way, for both urban and rural residents. Soviet city life is similar to life in Western cities fifty years ago. People live in crowded apartments, use public transportation, wear drab clothing, and eat a starchy diet. At the same time, medical care and other social services are better supplied now in the USSR than they were five decades ago in the West. Soviet rural life compares with still earlier European experience, but the presence of large machinery and trucks hampers comparison. The general pattern in both city and country is still

From cover of *Krokodil* No. 2, January 1975. Reprinted by permission of Sovfoto/Eastfoto.

*You never used to be late!*
*But I didn't used to have a car!*

"old-fashioned," yet elements of modernization run all through it.

Americans visiting the USSR for the first time are not envious of the general living standard of Soviet citizens. But many are surprised that conditions are as good as they appear to be. Visitors who have previously seen the USSR in the 1930s, 1940s, or early 1950s are genuinely impressed by the substantial and vivid contrast between former penury and present well-being.

Detailed comparisons of the goods and services available to the Soviet citizen and those available in the West would range widely from certain items in which the USSR already matches or exceeds the West, to the other extreme where it seems unlikely that the USSR will ever catch up. For example, subway, bus, and trolley service in Moscow now is far better than it is in New York City, and as good as in most European cities. On the other hand, in spite of large construction efforts since 1957, Soviet city people are scarcely as well provided with apartments as Westerners have been since 1900. The era of individual homes in the suburbs is not even visible on the Soviet horizon, except for a handful of the elite. Between these extremes are items such as television sets, where within a decade or so the USSR may have caught up with the West. If the share of Soviet GNP devoted to consumption were to rise, this catching-up process for most items could be accomplished more quickly. But regardless of the speed involved, state policy will favor communal forms of consumption, in place of what the Party considers to be blatantly individualistic.

The Soviet people travel to work by bus, trolley, train, or subway or on foot. Long-distance travel is by train or air (occasionally by bus). Automobiles have long been available for officials and the tourist services, but annual domestic production of cars passed the one million mark only in 1974 and the present total stock of 6 million cars for 254 million people compares with a U.S. stock of 109 million cars for 213 million people. The Soviet road situation is even less developed. There are now about 50,000 miles of paved (concrete or asphalt) highway in the USSR, compared with some 1.5 million miles in the United States. What does this contrast imply for Soviet prospects?

**Economic freedom**  Soviet citizens can choose freely among the goods and services available for consumption. Consumer choice is not, however, consumer sovereignty. Demand strong enough to empty shelves at existing prices will not induce producers to supply more, if the party has higher-priority uses for the inputs involved. The State-controlled production process moves forward under the influence of State investment and defense demands that override household needs. In other words, neither the commodity composition nor the broad proportions of Soviet production is subject to effective influence by the Soviet people.

In selecting a career, Soviet citizens have usually had wide freedom of choice, within certain limits. Many training opportunities are open. Quitting one job and taking another, perhaps in another part of the country, has been relatively easy, except during the 1940–53 period. Here again, however, party policy rather than personal bent ultimately decides how many musicians, engineers, machinists, or airline stewardesses will find training and job openings. There is ample scope for individual talents to the extent that they serve the national interest as seen by the Party.

For some twenty years, millions of Soviet citizens worked as slaves in corrective labor camps, but after 1953 most survivors were amnestied and now the camps hold only criminals and an unknown number of political prisoners. At present, people without regular salaried jobs are heckled as "parasites" and can be sent to another part of the country to reform their ways in labor colonies. For the normally employed, it is hazardous to bring pressure for better wages and working conditions. Soviet trade unions stress the interests of the State more than the interests of their members.

Thus, economic freedom is circumscribed in the USSR. One can earn a living, at State-approved tasks, and serve society, in State-approved ways, enjoying such rewards as are approved by the State. The politico-technical elite that makes these judgments is subject neither to market pressures nor to being voted out of office. And there is no private sector to provide employment to Soviet citizens who for any reason are denied access to governmental jobs. As we shall see when we examine the United States, the U.S. citizen, voting with both dollars and ballots, has far greater economic freedom than his Soviet counterpart.

**Economic justice**    Abundant opportunities for education and occupational training have given upward social mobility to millions of Soviet citizens since the 1920s. There has been discrimination against children of the former upper classes and of purge victims, together with markedly unfavorable treatment of the rural population as compared to urbanites; but equality of opportunity has been a major characteristic of Soviet society. This has not, however, meant equal incomes.

Marx predicted that under full communism each would be rewarded according to *need*. Until that happy day it would be necessary to reward each according to his *work*. From 1931 to the late 1950s, the principle of payment according to work was applied with a vengeance in the USSR. Wages were set by the State to reward hard work and improved skill. Pay by the piece was far more typical than pay by the hour. Bonuses for producing more than one's quota were numerous and substantial. As a result, wage rates and annual incomes became highly unequal, more so than in the West. But a wage reform put through during the late 1950s established standard base rates for all industries and occupations, plus geographic and skill differentials, creating a uniform system with much less inequality in it. Moreover, minimum wages were raised on two occasions in the late 1960s, thus further reducing the spread from low to high wage and salary incomes.

Large property incomes, enjoyed by individuals in many non-communist countries, do not exist in the USSR; hence this source of inequality is absent. But high positions in the USSR carry perquisites that have some of the same effects: cars with chauffeurs; special access to apartments, summer cottages, and rest homes; long holidays; and trips abroad.

Although reduction of regional inequalities has been a Soviet intention ever since 1917, progress has been slow. Backward minority groups have been brought forward, and outlying regions have been stimulated, yet many strong groups and central areas have more than held their relative position. Generally speaking, the three Baltic republics and nearby regions in the northwest have shown output growth rates above the national average since 1950, while territories in the southeast have grown at less than average rates. Since population growth rates are more rapid in Soviet Central Asia and the Caucasus (Moslem areas) than in the northwest, per-capita income differences seem to be widening still further.

**Economic stability and security**   Soviet citizens have a large measure of economic security. Jobs have been easy to get since 1930. The State has provided medical care and paid sick leaves, leaves for child-bearing, disability benefits, and retirement pensions. But the social security system is not notably generous by Western standards. The jobs available are not always ones the worker wants. Workers in seasonal occupations may spend weeks or months without earnings, but since temporary unemployment is not recognized, the States does nothing to maintain their income. Officially, "he who does not work, neither shall he eat." Absences from work for medical treatment require a doctor's certificate, and for many years these were sparingly granted. Protection against occupational injury is impaired by the lack of safety equipment in Soviet industry. Old age pensions before 1956 were so far below the average wage that little real support was provided. The various social insurance benefits were not made available to collective farm members, still 35 percent of the labor force, until 1964.

Pensions now range from 100 percent of the previous wage earned, for workers who earned the minimum wage of about $75 a month, down to 50 percent of earnings for those who received about $200 a month. Pensions can begin at age 60 for men and 55 for women (five years earlier for those in "difficult" work and ten years earlier for those in "dangerous" work). Invalids and others unable to support themselves are adequately provided for, and special pensions can be granted for outstanding national contributions.

General price stability is another feature of the Soviet system. Over the last twenty years the cost of living has risen very little, since retail prices are set by the State; upward pressure leads to disappearance of low-price lines or to loss of quality rather than to higher price tags. Meanwhile, money incomes have been rising substantially throughout the economy, so real disposable incomes have steadily improved,[1] without, however, setting off a wage–price spiral. In addition, as noted earlier, the international price changes of the early 1970s have helped rather than hurt Soviet foreign trade, so the internal price level has not been pushed up by worsened terms of trade.

Soviet economic stability comes from keeping demand chronically pressing on supply so that imbalances take the form of shortages rather than slack. Customers line up for desirable consumer goods and services; retail clerks are inattentive; untold hours of shoppers' time are spent trying to find supplies. The State economizes on retail services at the expense of the individual. In market economies where supply responds readily to demand, customer convenience is maximized, but some oversupply and idleness is a constant danger for producers and employees. We leave it to the reader to define an optimum in this area.

**Economic growth**  Soviet economic growth has been rapid but uneven. World Wars I and II brought twelve and ten years, re-

[1] See David W. Bronson and Barbara S. Severin, "Soviet Consumer Welfare," in U.S. Congress, Joint Economic Committee, *Soviet Economic Prospects for the Seventies* (1973), pp. 376–403.

spectively, of decline and recovery without net growth. From 1928 to 1940 and from 1950 to date, parts of the economy have grown very rapidly, while other sectors have grown slowly if at all. The total Soviet net national product grew, from 1928 to 1940 and again from 1950 to 1958, at about 7 percent per year. Industrial output grew at about 10 percent annually during these periods. But agricultural output fell in the 1930s and had scarcely recovered by 1940. From 1950 to 1958, by contrast, it rose almost 7 percent annually.

During the prewar industrial drive, living standards fell sharply in the early 1930s, recovered through 1937, and then fell back slightly with the onset of purges and the outbreak of war. The average real wage outside agriculture in 1940 was only 54 percent of the 1928 real wage, but 15 million people had migrated from low-income rural work to higher-income nonagricultural jobs, and 5 million urban persons entered the labor force. Between 1928 and 1940, the proportion of the labor force working outside agriculture rose from 18 to 41 percent. The shift brought real per capita consumption in 1940, averaged over the whole population, back roughly to the 1928 level.

Real wages and consumption rose rapidly and steadily after the mid-1940s, regaining the 1940 level around 1950 and reaching a level by 1958 that was just over twice what it had been in 1928, on a per capita basis. Both agricultural and nonagricultural incomes rose, and the continued shift of labor toward industry brought the share of the labor force outside agriculture to 51 percent in 1959.

The contrast between the 1928–40 period and the post-1950 period is startling. Before World War II, efforts were focused on building military power; life was grim. It became grimmer during the war, but the Soviet Union survived and recovered. In the 1950s, especially after the death of Stalin, growth spread to the agricultural sector and the output of consumer goods rose almost as rapidly as industrial output. Recently, as we have seen, growth has slowed down in the industrial sector and has been quite sporadic in agriculture. Real per capita consumption gains have continued, however, at a very respectable rate. Figure 5-1 shows output trends since 1952.

Further Soviet output growth will be spurred by the regime's undiminished urge to overtake and surpass the advanced countries of the West. Although the Soviet public now displays some concern for environmental disruption, so far it is not restraining industrial expansion. A large railroad construction project in eastern Siberia, for example, will spread half a million construction workers and their equipment across delicate Arctic territory, but the ecological consequences are cheerfully being risked. Clearly, billions of rubles of investment in housing, water mains, sewers, roads, and retail service facilities will be needed to fill the current gaps in Soviet modernization. Soviet military outlays, like those of the United States, continue to grow. Finally, with the population growing by 1 percent a year, additional needs and additional output potential are both brought into being.

## SUGGESTED READINGS

Campbell, Robert W., *The Soviet-Type Economies: Performance and Evolution*, 3rd ed. Boston: Houghton Mifflin, 1974.

> A very clear and interesting introduction to the USSR and Eastern Europe with some attention to China and Cuba.

Gregory, Paul R. and Robert C. Stuart, *Soviet Economic Structure and Performance*. New York: Harper & Row, 1974.

> A thorough and reliable textbook.

US Congress, Joint Economic Committee, *Soviet Economic Prospects for the Seventies*. Washington: Government Printing Office, 1973.

> Thirty papers by specialists reviewing the situation.

# THE EUROPEAN COMMUNITY

# 6

One of the newest of the world's economies, the European Community is also one of its largest and wealthiest. Its population of more than 260 million is 50 million greater than that of the United States and about 10 million greater than that of the Soviet Union. Its GNP, although only two-thirds that of the United States, is twice the USSR's and treble Japan's. Since its inception as a Community of Six (now Nine) in 1958, it has grown steadily, at times markedly. As a new combination of old parts, the Community is cranky and awkward, its future promising but uncertain.

## THE COMMUNITY'S ORGANIZATION AND STRUCTURE

**Origin and scope**   Ever since the collapse of the Holy Roman Empire more than 1000 years ago, philosophers and kings have dreamed and written of a peacefully united Europe. Encompassing only a portion of the European continent and considerably less than a unified political economy in the full sense, the European Community is not the dream come true. But it appears to be an important step in that direction.

Because the Community bears some resemblance to the age-old vision, its date of actual conception is hard to fix. As good a date as any is 1947, when, in response to the invitation of U.S. Secretary of State George C. Marshall, the war-ravaged states of Western Europe formed themselves into the Organization for European Economic Cooperation for purposes of planning and managing their reconstruction with massive American financial assistance. A second section of the Community's foundation was laid in 1948, when the so-called Benelux group (Belgium, The Netherlands, and Luxembourg) erected a customs union and thereby both eliminated most trade barriers among themselves and established a common set of barriers against nonmembers. The next step was especially dramatic: Under the guidance and prodding of two brilliant European federalists, Jean Monnet (then France's chief economic planner) and Robert Schumann (then France's foreign minister), all of Europe's iron, steel, and coal resources—most notably including those of the two traditional enemies, Germany and France—were pooled in 1952 under a common authority designated the European Coal and Steel Community. Though labeled a community, the ECSC was candidly supranational in character and intended by its sires to be a stepping stone toward European federation.

Subsequent events demonstrated that the federalists' reach exceeded their grasp. A determined effort, strongly supported from the sidelines by the United States, to create a European Defense Community and beyond that a European Political Union ended in failure in the mid-1950s. Dismayed but still resolute, Monnet took a different tack, turning back from military and political federation to economics. Joined by like-minded statesmen in the Benelux group, he produced plans for a European Economic Community (EEC) and a European Atomic Energy Community (Euratom). Governed by a Council of Ministers appointed by member states rather than by a supranational authority, both were born under separate Treaties of Rome, signed in 1957 by six nations—France, Germany, Italy, Belgium, The Netherlands, and Luxembourg. Great Britain had been invited to join but refused, so it was a Community of Six that began to function on 1 January 1958.

In the ensuing fourteen years the Six made slow, sometimes painful, but steady progress toward creation of a genuine common market, especially in agreeing to abstain from doing things that impede intraregional trade. In the meantime, Great Britain and its other European trading partners—Norway, Denmark, Sweden, Switzerland, Austria, Portugal, Finland, and Iceland—formed themselves into a free-trade area which, like the EEC, abolished internal customs duties but which, unlike the EEC, had no common *external* tariff wall. By the early 1960s, however, Britain had reconsidered its position with respect to the now-prospering EEC and applied for membership. In 1963 and again in 1967 its application was vetoed by France under the presidency of Charles de Gaulle. By 1971, de Gaulle had left the scene and with the blessing of his successor, Georges Pompidou, France joined the other five charter members in negotiating the admittance to the Community, effective 1 January 1973, of Britain, Denmark, and Ireland. Norway was also offered admission in 1972 and signed the Treaty of Accession, but its agreement failed of ratification at home. The remaining six members of the free-trade area began negotiating close links with the Community of Nine.

Two other events of historical importance deserve brief mention. A major step toward the full blending of ECSC, Euratom, and EEC into one Community was taken in 1967 with the entry into force of the Merger Treaty under which separate governing bodies for the three Communities were replaced by a single one. Of much greater potential significance was the subsequent resolution by the Community's leaders at the Paris Summit of 1972 to "transform the whole complex of the relations of the member states" by achieving full economic and monetary union by 1980.

**Common institutions**   In outward appearance, the European Community is a superstate with executive, legislative, and judicial branches. Major policy decisions are reached by the Council of Ministers, a nine-member body with representatives appointed by each of the member governments. The thirteen-member European Commission, whose responsibility is to the Community rather than to any member state, drafts proposed policies for the approval of the Council and assures their execution, once approved, in full accordance with the Community's treaties, laws, and regulations. There is a European Parliament with 198 seats, filled by persons drawn from national parliaments of the Community's membership and endowed with consultative privileges and authority to remove the Commission from power on a vote of censure. There is also a nine-member Court of Justice, one judge by appointment from each nation in the Community, with sole jurisdiction over matters of the Community's law and to which individuals, companies, institutions of the Community, and member governments may appeal.

As even this abbreviated sketch makes clear, the actual distribution of power and authority among the four institutions of governance is very unequal. The Parliament is essentially an advisory, as opposed to a legislative, body and the Court lacks the capacity to impose legal sanctions against an offender. In reality, therefore, the institutions that drive the European Community toward its short- and long-range objectives are the Council and the Commission.

In the early years of the European Community, when the federalists held sway and the Community was regarded as the embryo of a European superstate, the Commission and its Brussels-based staff of "Eurocrats" dominated the scene, primarily by utilizing what was called "its own power of decision" to initiate policies. It behaved, that is, as if it were the European Community's motor, without which the Community would be little more than an intergovernmental organization that would disintegrate as soon as its members fell into serious disagreement. For a number of reasons, including but not limited to members' nationalism, the Commission's aggressiveness was in due course curbed and the Council's primacy made clear. That is the situation at present.

There is more to the European Community's political structure than its official agencies. It also includes a mixture of private groups and organizations that transcend national boundaries—international business enterprises, international associations of farmers, trade unionists, scientists, professional civil servants.

> Bits and pieces of the national governments are themselves part of the system; so are some of the parliaments. . . . If . . . this is more like a bag of marbles than a melting-pot, the marbles are soft on the surface and made of some sticky substance, like putty, which keeps them clinging together as they are pushed around and constantly make contact with one another inside the bag. . . . [It] certainly is not very coherent. It is much less satisfactory to describe than the simplified version of a supranational European government which was the ideal of the founding fathers of the Community.[1]

**Common policies**   There are many reasons why the European Community should not even exist. It includes, after all, nine well-established, proudly sovereign states, with the youngest over 100 years of age and some that date back several centuries. The peoples of Western Europe speak six different languages (French, German, Italian, Dutch, Danish, and English), not to mention dialectical variations in each, and they daily conduct business in nine different currencies, exclusive of "foreign" monies (for exam-

[1] Andrew Shonfield, *Europe: Journey to an Unknown Destination* (London: Allen Lane, 1973), p. 17.

ple, the U.S. dollar) that regularly circulate. And there are profound differences among Europe's nationalities and ethnic groups
with respect to values, traditions and customs, and laws—differences that have upon several occasions in the past caused two or
more of them to go to war against each other. Indeed, these
differences still provoke eruptions within the Community, threat-
ening its very survival.

What ingredients are in the cement that has so far not only
held the Community together but enabled it to enlarge? The list
of factors is long, but two stand out: (1) all members' recognition of their mutual self-interest in a thriving, Western European
economy large enough to compete with the United States and
stand up to the USSR, and (2) their common reliance upon the
market mechanism as the means for allocating scarce resources
and for distributing incomes. In other words, each member recog-
nizes that its economic well-being varies directly with its ability
to conduct trade with the others, and each (although in varying
degrees) accepts the primacy of private consumers and producers
in economic decision-making.

Upon this foundation have been established a number of common policies and programs that are carried out by Community,
rather than national, institutions. The common activities em-
body a positive set of economic and social objectives—in particular, balanced economic development, higher living standards,
closer relations among the peoples of Europe, and expansion of
world trade. They include specifically:

1. The customs union and the common external tariff. The
creation of the customs union, described by the Community itself
as the cornerstone of the edifice, removed all intra-Community
tariffs, quotas, and legal and administrative barriers to trade. The
common external tariff applies a unified set of duties upon goods
imported by all members from the rest of the world.

2. Common agricultural policy (CAP). Designed to create
a common market for farm products, the CAP's main features are
free trade in agricultural produce; common price supports to raise
and maintain farmers' incomes, coupled with "variable levies" at
the Community's frontiers, which adjust the prices of imported
farm products to the prevailing level of support prices in the Community; and a long-term, jointly financed plan to modernize farming and consolidate landholdings that are too small to be efficient.
The European Agricultural Guidance and Guarantee Fund covers

expenditures to support farm prices, pay export refunds, and promote agricultural modernization. The fund is financed from the Community's general funds, which come in part from duties on imports from outside the Community.

3. Economic and monetary union. Simple logic suggests, and ample experience demonstrates, that the survival and growth of the Common Market depends heavily upon the maintenance of stable, although not necessarily unchanging, relationships among the national economies and currencies of the members. In a series of steps beginning with the transformation of the immediate postwar period's European Payments Union into today's European Monetary Cooperation Fund (which helps to finance and coordinate currency exchange-rate interventions), the Community has committed itself in principle to creation of a full economic and monetary union by 1980, perhaps with a common currency.

4. Social policy. From its start the European Community has pursued a policy (that became fully effective in 1968) of enabling workers to move freely among partner countries in search of job opportunities while retaining social security benefits and rights regardless of where they work. The Community has also striven to assure that workers are protected from the adverse consequences of structural and other changes and are helped to adjust to new jobs. Matching contributions are made by member countries and the ECSC to pay for retraining and relocation of coal miners and steel workers. A similar arrangement obtains between member nations and the European Social Fund for workers in other sectors.

5. Regional policy. The Community is pocked with regions, the largest and most notorious of which is southern Italy (the Mezzogiorno), that have large amounts of unused and underused resources. In pursuit of what the European Community calls "a better regional balance," several Community-wide institutions make loans to attract new industries to these areas and to provide them with modern transportation and communications facilities, among other things. Chief among the bodies now playing this role are the European Social Fund, the European Investment Bank, and the European Agricultural Fund. Just joining the effort is the Regional Development Fund, financed from the Community's own resources.

6. Industrial policy. Although the elimination of tariffs and quotas among the Nine was a major step toward creation of a unified market, other obstacles to free internal trade remain. They

© 1974 Punch (Rothco).

*"He's as arrogant as the Germans, difficult as the French, volatile as the Italians, blunt as the Dutch, dour as the Danes and as contrary as the Irish, in fact, a true European!"*

include national differences in labor and industrial laws and regulations, imposed in the name of public health, safety, environmental protection, or "fair competition"; long-standing unwillingness of many European businessmen to abandon their "live-and-let-live" attitude in favor of vigorous market rivalry; persistent consumer loyalty to "national" goods; national governments' favoritism to domestic suppliers in the award of public contracts; and discriminatory national tax policies that hinder cross-frontier mergers and transfers of capital and profit. The European Commission is alive to the need to attack these obstacles and is pressing for early adoption of a common industrial policy. Also in the process of development are common policies for energy, technological research, transportation, and environmental protection.

7. Common tax policy. Indirect taxes, or levies imposed upon consumption expenditures and property as opposed to personal or business income, are the primary source of internal revenue in western Europe, accounting on the average for about 60 percent of each economy's governmental receipts; in the United States, by contrast, the proportion is only 40 percent. Among the forms of indirect taxation imposed by the Community's members, the most

important is the turnover tax, an impost that is added to the prices of taxable products whether they are produced and sold at home or imported for domestic sale. Only goods produced and exported are exempted from the turnover tax.

In the absence of a common method of taxation and similar tax rates, establishment and maintenance of free, undistorted competition among Community members—a major objective of the Common Market—would be unattainable. For instance, if a higher tax were imposed upon imports than upon comparable home-produced products, the difference would have the same protective effect as the customs duties that have been abolished. Equally, if there are intermember differences in the rebate of tax on exports, some sellers in the Community would receive, in fact although not in name, an export subsidy, which the rules of the Market forbid.

To eliminate these fiscal distortions of competition, the Council of Ministers in 1967 voted to institute a common turnover tax system based on the value-added method of taxation; foot-dragging has so far prevented its implementation. Harmonization of the tax rates among the Nine will take place after the common system is established. Also in the planning stage are programs to harmonize excise duties and direct taxes and to eliminate international double taxation of interest and dividends.

8. Consumer protection. The European Commission protects consumers against "unfair" trading practices through enforcement of common rules to maintain competition. In 1972, for example, it fined sixteen leading sugar producers approximately $10 million for operating a cartel; and it fined a group of sound-recording companies and glass-insulating-material producers for restrictive practices.

9. External relations. In addition to their common customs tariff, the Nine have a common antidumping[2] policy and a common procedure for quotas. Through Association Agreements with developing countries that once were colonies of France, Belgium, Italy, the Netherlands, and Great Britain, the Community provides tariff concessions and, through its European Development Fund, financial and technical assistance. Beginning in 1971, it also instituted a worldwide system of generalized tariff preferences that now applies to 90 developing countries.

[2] Dumping is the practice of selling abroad at prices below delivered cost.

# ECONOMIC SIMILARITIES AND DISSIMILARITIES

Viewed as a totality, the European Community is an impressive economy. Within its land expanse of nearly 600,000 square miles is contained a rich and varied endowment of natural resources—arable land, fresh water, minerals, forests, and fisheries. The stock of social overhead capital—transportation and communications facilities, health-care and school systems, electric power networks, and so forth—is both sizable and modern. The stock of directly productive capital in agriculture, industry, and services and government is similarly large and up to date. Perhaps most important, the labor force as a whole is well educated, well trained, and vigorous.

Although the Community's natural resources have been exploited intensively for many decades, they continue to support a high volume of agricultural and industrial production. For example, 98 percent or more of the Community's consumption of wheat, fresh vegetables, meat, poultry, and dairy products is produced within its own borders; and well over 80 percent of its annual consumption of other grains, white sugar, and fresh fruit (excluding citrus) is internally produced. Despite steady depletion of its iron ore and coal reserves, the Community is the world's largest producer of steel. It is also the world's leader in production of plastics and cement.

The main natural resource the Community lacks in significant measure is oil, which is its main source of energy and also the basic input of many of its industrial products, such as plastics, synthetic fibers, and fertilizer. Most of its oil comes from suppliers in North Africa and the Middle East; pools recently discovered in the North Sea are likely at best to meet only Britain's needs. As the Arab oil embargo during late 1973 and early 1974 dramatically demonstrated, a prolonged reduction in the availability of imported petroleum would drastically cut the Community's level of economic activity.

The Community's major source of wealth is its human population and especially the two-fifths that are in the labor force. Although its total population of more than 260 million is one of the world's largest, it is now growing at a comparatively sedate rate. The crude birth rate has stabilized at 16 per 1,000, the crude death rate at roughly 11 per 1,000, so the natural rate of increase is 0.5 percent yearly. Compared to those elsewhere in the world, the

Community's indigenous labor force is of high quality: the great majority are not only functionally literate, they also have the education[3] and the training to perform highly complex tasks. Just as important, the workers as a whole are, by any reasonable standard of comparison, well fed, well clothed, well housed, and well cared for medically.

Although the nine economies of the Community have much in common, they differ from one another in several important respects. Certain of these differences deserve special, if brief, mention.

**Level and rates of growth**  Measured by total output (Table 6-1), the European Community is divided broadly into two groups: four "big" economies (Germany, France, the United Kingdom, and Italy) and five "small" ones (the Netherlands, Belgium, Denmark, Ireland, and Luxembourg). The picture changes markedly, however, if output per capita is the yardstick. Denmark, France, Germany, Luxembourg, and Belgium constitute the "big five" with amounts ranging from $3,200 to $3,700; the Netherlands and the United Kingdom fall into a middle-sized category with a range of $2,600 to $2,800; and Italy ($2,000) and Ireland ($1,600) are at the bottom.

The data in Table 6-1 reveal yet a third set of groupings in growth rates per capita during 1952–73. Germany, France, and Italy headed the list with rates above 4 percent yearly, followed by Denmark, Belgium, the Netherlands, Ireland, and Luxembourg, each with rates in the range 3.1–3.8 percent. The laggard was the United Kingdom (2.1 percent).

A number of other noteworthy points emerge from the table. Four of the founding Six (Luxembourg and Belgium are the exceptions) enjoyed annual growth rates of both GNP and GNP per capita that were significantly higher than those of the three that joined the Community in 1973. The German economy grew substantially more between 1952 and 1973 than the other eight; as a result, Germany displaced the United Kingdom as the Community's largest economy. Comparison of France and the United Kingdom is particularly impressive: In 1952 the French GNP was roughly 20 percent less than Britain's, whereas in 1973 it was

---

[3] The mean length of schooling for the Community is nearly ten years, about one year less than in the United States.

## TABLE 6-1
### Changes in Gross Domestic Product, Population, and GDP Per Capita, for the Nine Members of the European Community, 1952 and 1973

| COUNTRY | GROSS DOMESTIC PRODUCT (billion Eur[a] at 1963 prices) | | | POPULATION (thousands) | | | GROSS DOMESTIC PRODUCT PER CAPITA (1963 Eur[a]) | | |
|---|---|---|---|---|---|---|---|---|---|
| | 1952 | 1973 | ANNUAL PERCENT GROWTH | 1952 | 1973 | ANNUAL PERCENT GROWTH | 1952 | 1973 | ANNUAL PERCENT GROWTH |
| Germany | 44,500 | 152,000 | 6.0 | 47,728 | 61,974 | 1.3 | 930 | 2,450 | 4.7 |
| France | 49,100 | 145,300 | 5.3 | 42,460 | 52,143 | 1.0 | 1,160 | 2,790 | 4.3 |
| United Kingdom | 61,500 | 112,500 | 2.9 | 50,737 | 56,021 | 0.5 | 1,210 | 2,010 | 2.4 |
| Italy | 26,400 | 78,800 | 5.4 | 47,666 | 54,898 | 0.7 | 550 | 1,440 | 4.6 |
| Netherlands | 8,700 | 25,100 | 5.2 | 10,380 | 13,438 | 1.2 | 840 | 1,870 | 3.4 |
| Belgium | 9,200 | 21,200 | 4.1 | 8,725 | 9,742 | 0.5 | 1,050 | 2,180 | 3.5 |
| Denmark | 5,100 | 12,900 | 4.5 | 4,336 | 5,027 | 0.7 | 1,180 | 2,570 | 3.8 |
| Ireland | 1,700 | 3,400 | 3.4 | 2,953 | 3,051 | 0.2 | 580 | 1,110 | 3.2 |
| Luxembourg | 400 | 900 | 3.9 | 300 | 353 | 0.8 | 1,330 | 2,550 | 3.1 |
| Nine-Member Community | 206,600 | 552,100 | 4.8 | 215,285 | 256,647 | 0.8 | 960 | 2,150 | 3.9 |

[a] The Eur is the standard unit of monetary account for the Community.

SOURCE: Derived from estimates in Statistical Office of the European Communities, *National Accounts Aggregates, 1951–1972* (Luxembourg, 1973), and *1960–1973* (Luxembourg, 1974).

nearly 30 percent greater. And although France's population grew twice as fast as the United Kingdom's, French GNP per capita rose by about 140 percent while Britain's rose by only 66 percent. Notable, too, is the fact that, despite its small area and population, Denmark headed the Nine in size of GNP per capita in 1952 and was second to France in 1973.

**Output and employment by economic sector**   The figures in Table 6-2 substantiate the fact that the Community as a whole has progressed well beyond the stage in which agriculture is predominant. Only 5 percent of the European Community's gross domestic product originates in agriculture (which includes forestry and fishing), and less than 10 percent of its civilian workers are employed in that sector; the proportions for industry are 45 percent (roughly estimated) and 44 percent, respectively. These figures are broadly comparable with those for the United States, where

**TABLE 6-2**
**Gross Domestic Product at Factor Costs by Sector**
**and Civilian Labor Force by Sector,**
**European Community, 1971 (in percentages)**

|  | AGRICULTURE[a] | | INDUSTRY[b] | | SERVICES[c] | |
|---|---|---|---|---|---|---|
|  | GDP | CLF[d] | GDP | CLF[d] | GDP | CLF[d] |
| Germany (F.R.) | 3.5 | 8.3 | 51.4 | 49.2 | 45.2 | 41.8 |
| France | 6.3 | 13.2 | —[e] | 39.6 | N.A. | 45.0 |
| United Kingdom | 2.9 | 2.7 | 43.3 | 44.3 | 53.8 | 50.1 |
| Italy | 9.8 | 18.9 | 38.7 | 42.7 | 51.6 | 35.2 |
| Netherlands | 5.7 | 6.9 | 41.8 | 37.7 | 52.5 | 53.9 |
| Belgium | 4.2 | 4.4 | 43.7 | 43.4 | 52.2 | 50.3 |
| Denmark | 7.5 | 10.9 | 38.7 | 37.6 | 53.8 | 51.5 |
| Ireland | 16.4 | 24.9 | 35.6 | 29.0 | 48.0 | 40.0 |
| Luxembourg | 4.4 | 10. | 57.5 | 47.3 | 38.1 | 42.6 |
| European Community | 5.3 | 9.9 | — | 43.7 | — | 44.3 |

[a] Includes forestry and fishing.
[b] Includes mining and construction.
[c] Includes general government.
[d] Excludes unemployed workers.
[e] Data not available.

SOURCE: Eurostat, *Basic Statistics of the Community*, 1972, pp. 23, 26.

the proportion in agriculture is 4 percent and in industry 27 percent (see p. 168).

These aggregates conceal important intra-Community differences. The data in Table 6-2 show, for example, that four of the Nine are above the Community's average in share of gross domestic product originating in agriculture. In two of these cases, Ireland and Italy, the relatively high percentages bespeak serious structural problems in the national economy (discussed below). Denmark and France, in contrast, have thriving agricultural sectors. France, in fact, is the Community's "bread basket": Containing nearly half the European Community's total farming area, it produces a third or more of the Community's combined output of wheat and other cereals, sugar beets, and dairy products.

Climate and geography partially explain France's comparative advantage, particularly with respect to Germany and Italy, both heavy food importers. Also in France's favor is the fact that the average size of its farms is nearly 50 acres, whereas in Italy it is less than 27 acres and in Germany only 17 acres.

> Worse still, despite steps taken to consolidate farm holdings, many properties are spread over several plots of land, sometimes with considerable distances between them. The ridiculous extreme is in Germany, where the average holding comprises about eight different sites, each averaging less than . . . 3 acres.[4]

How do these small, usually high-cost farms stay in operation? Why don't they succumb to market forces, thereby freeing labor and capital for employment in other sectors where their marginal products would be higher? To a considerable extent, that process has been going on for many years; between 1950 and the early 1970s, the farming population of the original Six fell from 20 million to under 10 million. Furthermore, the Community in 1971 adopted the so-called Mansholt Plan, which was designed to reduce still further the number of farms through compensation from Community funds to those who move out of agriculture entirely or at least remove acreage from production.

Even so, there are institutional barriers to full-scale rationalization of Europe's agriculture. In particular, acting in the belief that

[4] Roger Broad and R. J. Garrett, *Community Europe Today* (London: Oswald Wolfe, 1972), p. 90.

forced depopulation of the farming sector would be contrary to their national interests, several member governments have insisted upon the establishment and maintenance of a Common Agricultural Policy, the substance of which is a Community-wide system of price supports and export subsidies frankly designed as an umbrella over high-cost farms and farmers.

Currently, CAP is a costly burden upon the Community's consumers. It is not likely to remain so much longer; price supports will probably become unnecessary. Worldwide demand for agricultural products seems sure to make all of the Community's future output marketable at prices that will transform most or all of today's submarginal farms into profitable enterprises.

Excepting Ireland, which still has a relatively undeveloped industrial base, and Luxembourg, which is heavily specialized in crude-steel production, each of the Community's members—and thus the Community as a whole—has a well-established, diversified manufacturing sector. Underpinning this sector, as has already been observed, are a still-abundant supply of natural resources and a large pool of skilled labor. Moreover, much of the Community's aggregate stock of plant and equipment is of recent vintage and technologically up to date, a condition substantially attributable to the region's massive effort after 1945 (with U.S. aid) to replace the industrial capital that had worn out or been destroyed during the preceding period of severe economic depression and war. The European Community is, as a result, either the world's leader or among the leaders in the production of intermediate goods (for example, crude pig iron, crude steel, finished rolled steel products, cement, chemicals), producers' durables (light and heavy engineering equipment, electrical and electronic equipment), consumer durables (automobiles, domestic appliances), and consumer nondurables (textile and leather apparel).

Although alive and in respectable health, the Community's industrial sector is not trouble-free. What most holds it back from vigorous maturity is the lack of an internal market large enough for European enterprises fully to exploit modern production and distribution methods that would enable them to compete effectively at home and abroad with the transnational corporations based in the United States and Japan. The latter enterprises, which include IBM, Exxon, General Motors, Ford, Mitsui, and Toyota, have established bridgeheads within the Community either by acquiring assets of European firms or establishing wholly owned subsidiaries. They have seized a sizable share of the intra-Community market through exploitation of their superiority in technology, financial resources, and marketing ability. As was suggested earlier, a main purpose of the emerging Common Industrial Policy—especially those elements designed to facilitate cross-frontier mergers, promote joint ventures, and stimulate European scientific and technological development—is to enable European concerns to regain the markets they have lost.

**Regional disparities**   Unlike a rising tide, economic growth raises some boats in the harbor but not all. In the Common Market's case, a decade of vigorous postwar reconstruction and expansion still left it, at its founding in 1958, with a condition in which the value of the average output per person in its mostly highly developed regions was at least three times the average in its economically distressed areas. It was because of these regional variations that the Treaty of Rome set the objective of "reducing the disparities between [sic] the various regions and mitigating the backwardness of the less favored areas."

The regions of the European Community classified as in distress are of two broad types. One is the primarily agricultural area that remains seriously underdeveloped, the other the area where the main industries are in decline because of structural changes (shifts in consumer demand, technological obsolescence, and so on). Notable among the underdeveloped areas of the Community is the southern half of Italy, the Mezzogiorno; large segments of northwestern (Brittany, lower Normandy), southwestern (Languedoc, Roussillon, Pyrenees, and Aquitaine), and central (Massif Central) France; the Scottish highlands; and rural Ireland. Among the areas hardest hit by structural change are the coal-mining areas in Britain, France, Belgium, and Germany.

All of the Nine have addressed themselves, individually and as a group through Community-wide organizations, to the eradication of these pockets of poverty. Some progress has been recorded. Thanks, for example, to substantial investment expenditures by the Italian government together with the European Investment Bank and various private enterprises, the gross product in the Mezzogiorno rose at an average annual rate of 5 percent between 1951 1971. The experience in southern Italy also exemplifies the stubbornness of the underdevelopment problem: Despite impressive growth over two decades, the region's net per capita income in 1971 was only two-thirds of the national average, and although it contains 38 percent of Italy's population, it still contributed only 25 percent of the nation's income.[5]

## THE COMMUNITY'S ECONOMIC PERFORMANCE

It is too early at this writing to evaluate the performance of the Common Market of Nine. The Six, however, have been grouped together for upward of 20 years, so they will be the focus of our assessment effort. As to that, it must be pointed out that because the Market is still much more an assemblage of national economies than a unified system, our review must go beyond measuring the degree to which it has produced plenty, freedom, equity, stability, and growth. Also to be judged is the contribution of the Community itself: Would similar or better performance in any or all respects have been forthcoming had it never been formed?

**Plenty** According to most of the customary indicators of material well-being, western Europeans lag well behind Americans (Table 6-3). Compared to the rest of the world, though, the Community's peoples are affluent indeed. And their position will continue to improve, absolutely if not relatively, as long as the growth rate in the Community exceeds the rate of growth of population, now only 0.5 percent yearly. The prospects for that are good.

To what extent has the Community as an institution contributed to Western Europe's growing affluence? Because the Community is only one of many factors impinging upon the individual economies, a precise answer cannot be given. It is all but certain, however, that some of the changes set in motion by the Treaty of Rome have contributed importantly to the rise in real income in all the original Six. Notable among these changes is the creation of a unified market that has (a) enabled a growing number of European concerns to realize economies of scale in production and distribution and thereby to sell their products at lower prices than otherwise, and (b) greatly diversified consumer choice among goods and services of nearly all kinds.

[5] European Investment Bank, *The European Investment Bank and the Problems of the Mezzogiorno,* 1972.

## TABLE 6-3
## Selected Indicators of Living Conditions,
## European Community and United States

|  | SIX-MEMBER COMMUNITY | NINE-MEMBER COMMUNITY | UNITED STATES |
|---|---|---|---|
| Food consumption, 1970[a] |  |  |  |
| Grain | 87 | 83 | 62 |
| Meat | 68 | 68 | 110 |
| Fish | 12 | —[e] | 5 |
| Milk and cream | 82 | 96 | 126 |
| Eggs | 14 | 14 | 18 |
| Vegetables | 115 | 100 | 92 |
| Fruit | 100 | —[e] | 56 |
| Cars in use, 1972[b] | 237 | 233 | 448 |
| Television sets in use, 1971[b] | 224 | 240 | 409 |
| Telephones in use, 1971[b] | 198 | 215 | 581 |
| Health services, 1970[c] |  |  |  |
| Physicians | 160 | —[e] | 149 |
| Pharmacists | 51 | —[e] | 61 |
| Hospital Beds | 969 | —[e] | 812 |
| Nonindustrial electricity consumption, 1971[d] | 1,175 | 1,437 | 4,230 |

[a] Kilograms (1 kg = 2.2 lb) per head per year.
[b] Number per 1,000 population.
[c] Number per 100,000 population.
[d] Kilowatt-hours per capita.
[e] Data not available.

SOURCE: Eurostat.

**Economic justice**   Reliable data on distribution of personal income are unobtainable for most of the world's economies. On the basis of the figures that do exist, fortified by impressionistic observations, it can be generalized that a substantial degree of inequality is the rule, not the exception, in command and market economies alike. In Western Europe, where there are data for several countries, the degree of inequality is strikingly large (Table 6-4). Wealth is distributed even more unequally.

### TABLE 6-4
### Percentage Shares of Total Personal Income
### Going to Percentile Population Groups,
### before Taxes, Selected Countries, 1962–64

|  | PERCENTILE OF POPULATION | | |
|---|---|---|---|
|  | TOP 10% | TOP 20% | LOWEST 10% |
| Denmark | 27.1 | 43.2 | 1.7 |
| France | 36.8 | 53.7 | 0.5 |
| Germany (F.R.) | 41.4 | 52.9 | 2.1 |
| Netherlands | 33.8 | 48.4 | 1.3 |
| United Kingdom | 29.3 | 44.2 | 2.0 |
| United States | 28.8 | 45.5 | 0.8 |

SOURCE: Richard B. DuBoff, *Economic Growth and Structural Change in Western Capitalism*, Warner Modular Publications, Module 8 (1973), p. 16.

These inequalities are being reduced to some extent by the policies and programs of the European Community. Note has already been taken of the regional development efforts that have been made in southern Italy and distressed areas elsewhere and of the attempt through the Common Agricultural Policy to raise and stabilize farmers' incomes. Nearly two million workers in declining industries have been retrained and relocated in better-paying jobs through Community procedures. The Community has made considerable progress toward its declared goal of equal pay for male and female workers in similar lines of work. Paid holidays for industrial workers in the European Community are much more numerous than in the United States. Hospital care throughout the Community is free, and all members pay family allowances.

Little is known about the degree of educational and employment opportunity in the Community. Scraps of data suggest, however, that (a) until recently there was only limited access, based on socioeconomic status, to the Community's institutions of higher education and through them to high-level professional, scientific, and managerial jobs; but (b) the barriers to access are being lowered all over the European Community. Equality of employment opportunity is also promoted by the Community's rules, which declare unequivocally that there shall be freedom of movement of labor among the member states as well as freedom to supply services and to establish commercial and industrial enterprises.

**Economic stability and security**  The Community gets mixed marks for its performance in the area of economic stabilization. On the one hand, in the entire period since 1958, none of the original Six has suffered a prolonged decline in gross domestic product and employment. In this respect the Community compares favorably with the United States, which experienced a severe recession in 1957–58 that lingered into 1960–61, went through a shorter but still painful downturn in 1969–70, and experienced a steep decline in 1974–75. On the other hand, the yearly rates of growth of gross domestic product in all Six were mildly irregular (Fig. 6-1), unemployment rose and fell perceptibly, consumer prices rose continuously and at the period's end very rapidly, and recurring balance-of-payments disequilibria kept the intra-Community structure of exchange rates under almost constant pressure (between 1958 and late 1971 the official value of the German mark was raised twice, while that of the French franc was reduced twice and the Dutch guilder once).

For the compelling reason that the Six refused fully to harmonize their national fiscal and monetary policies, much less create Community-wide institutions with powers in this area, the European Community as an entity had little or no impact upon economic stabilization policies and practices during 1958–72. At the end of the period, though, the members (now numbering nine) pledged to form themselves into a full economic and monetary union by 1980.

**Economic growth**  The Six's average annual rate of output growth of 5.1 percent during the 1960s and early 1970s almost deserves to be called spectacular, especially when it is compared with the figures for other highly developed economies such as the United States (4.3 percent) and the United Kingdom (2.9 percent). What factors best explain this impressive outcome? In particular, did the establishment of the Common Market contribute significantly?

Until all the relevant data are collected and analyzed rigorously, we can offer no definitive answer to either of these ques-

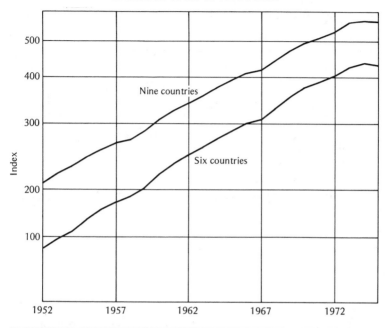

**FIG. 6-1**

**European Community Gross Domestic Product,
by Year, 1952–75,
in billions of Eur at 1963 Prices**

Nine countries

Six countries

Index

1952    1957    1962    1967    1972

tions. But enough is known already to support some intriguing testable hypotheses. For example, from his reading of the European experience from 1949 to 1963, Professor Charles Kindleberger has concluded that the expansion "followed what W. Arthur Lewis calls the model of 'growth with unlimited supplies of labor.' Lewis and others . . . have sought to apply the model to less developed countries. The model's most striking relevance, however, has been among the developed countries of Europe."[6] In support of this contention, Kindleberger musters evidence to the effect that the fastest-growing European economies were those with a large supply of labor. In the Netherlands the supply came from a high rate of natural increase; in Germany, France, and Italy, from transfers of workers from agriculture to industry and services. In

[6] Charles P. Kindleberger, *Europe's Postwar Growth: The Role of Labor Supply* (Cambridge, Mass.: Harvard University Press, 1967), p. 3.

France and Germany it also was due to immigration of unemployed and underemployed workers from the Mediterranean countries. Those countries with no substantial increase in the labor supply—notably, Belgium and Britain—have grown more slowly than the others.

The European Community, according to this thesis, played a supporting rather than a leading role. Its main contribution was to encourage intra-Community migration of labor from areas of surplus to areas of shortage. In the Community's early years, the outflow, especially from Italy, was very large. After the mid-1960s it diminished, chiefly because economic growth raised labor demand in all six nations of the Community. Germany and France then began importing workers from nonmember countries such as Yugoslavia and Turkey. Even so, as late as 1970–71 there were over a million Community nationals working in Community economies other than their own.

Kindleberger's hypothesis is partially supported by Edward

### TABLE 6-5
### Foreign Workers in Community Countries, 1970–71[a]

|  | ALL FOREIGN WORKERS | NATIONALS OF OTHER COMMUNITY MEMBERS[d] | FOREIGNERS AS PERCENT OF TOTAL WORK FORCE |
|---|---|---|---|
| Belgium (1970) | 208,000 | 117,000 | 5.5 |
| France (1970) | 1,200,000 | 280,000 | 5.8 |
| Germany (1971)[b] | 2,241,000 | 530,000 | 8.3 |
| Italy (1970) | 39,000 | 12,000 | 0.2 |
| Luxembourg (1970) | 33,000 | 26,000 | 23.0 |
| Netherlands (1971)[c] | 125,000 | 49,000 | 2.7 |
| Community | 3,487,000 | 1,015,000 | 5.1 |

[a] Annual averages.
[b] As of 30 September 1971.
[c] As of 15 March 1971.
[d] Mainly Italians.

SOURCE: European Communities Press and Information, "The Common Market and the Common Man," 4th ed., June 1972 (pamphlet), p. 7.

Denison's investigation of differences in growth rates in Europe and the United States during 1950–62.[7] Although Denison's period of study included only the first five years of the Common Market's existence, his findings are highly germane to our concerns. Summarized in a way that is unjust to Denison's sophisticated analysis, they are:

1. Gains from reallocation of resources from agriculture to other sectors "bear a large part of the burden of explaining growth rate differentials. All European countries except the United Kingdom, Belgium, and the Netherlands gained more than the United States by reducing the overallocations of resources to agriculture and all except the United Kingdom gained more by reducing the number of self-employed and unpaid family workers in nonagricultural industries."[8]

2. Reduction in barriers to international trade contributed only modestly to European Growth.

3. Economies of scale also contributed to European growth. In some degree, these economies stemmed from the removal of trade barriers and the consequent enlargement of sellers' markets. Of greater importance were scale economies made possible by income-induced expansion of purchases of products with high income elasticity. Previously the goods in point (such as automobiles and domestic appliances) were produced in small volume at high unit cost. As Europeans' incomes rose, so did their demand for income-elastic items—which, in turn, justified the increased scale of output that lowered unit costs and selling prices.

## THE COMMUNITY'S PROSPECTS

The European Community's record of economic progress in its first 15 years was remarkable. Its average annual rate of growth of gross national product, as has been said, exceeded 5 percent. Gross national product per capita, a better measure of improvement in individual well-being, rose in excess of 4 percent per year. Whereas world trade (measured by exports) trebled, and mutual trade among industrialized nations as a whole increased by roughly 150 percent, mutual trade among the original Six increased more than

[7] Edward F. Denison, *Why Growth Rates Differ: Postwar Experience in Nine Western Countries* (Washington: The Brookings Institution, 1967).
[8] *Ibid.*, p. 321.

sixfold and members' imports from the rest of the world more than doubled. Evidently, the Community has had "trade-creating" as well as "trade-diverting" effects. That is, although formation of the Market caused members to increase trade among themselves at the partial expense of nonmembers, growing incomes within the Market increased members' trade with non-Market economies.

The first 15 years were also notable politically. Old rivalries and enmities were greatly subdued, even if not put aside. Even in the middle 1960s, when the French refused for an 18-month period to take an active part in the Community's policy-making processes, the Community continued to carry on its daily business and—what is more important—preserved its hard-won integrity as well as its central institutions.

Under the best of circumstances, the next 15 years will be a far sterner testing time for the European Community than the first 15. Establishment of a customs union and common external tariff—the major task completed thus far—was relatively easy compared to creation of full economic and monetary union. Not only must a myriad of complex technical problems be solved on the road to union, but each member will have to surrender a substantial part of its national sovereignty, that is, submerge its national interest to the collective interest. That is the true meaning of "harmonization of fiscal, monetary, agricultural, commercial, industrial and developmental policies."

Judging from events since New Year's Day 1973, when the Six became Nine, the circumstances during the Community's second phase will be something less than the best. Throughout 1973 and 1974, all Nine, in only moderately differing degree, were victims of savage economic blows, the effects of which are likely to be long-lasting. Triggered by a combination of factors, notably rising worldwide demand associated with economic growth in many lands, annual rates of inflation in the European Community doubled or trebled; by mid-1975 prices were rising in Italy at a yearly rate of 20 percent, in Britain at 25 percent, in France at 14 percent. Concurrently, unemployment was rising steeply; foreign-exchange rates, hitherto limited to movement within a narrow range by concerted action of members' central banks, broke their bonds; and deficits in the balance of trade of Britain and Italy in particular zoomed to alarming proportions. Most ominous of all was the panicky breaking of ranks among the Nine when, faced in early 1974 with a politically motivated embargo upon their imports of petroleum from Arabian fields, several elected to bargain independently for adequate supplies of the essential fuel.

Economic historians of the future may well record that these events tempered the Nine's steel and thereby contributed materially to their subsequent achievement of full economic and monetary union. For this to be said, however, the Nine must promptly solve a number of serious problems. Heading the agenda is correction of the persisting tendency, especially in Italy and Britain, toward deficit in external trade. For all its indigenous wealth, the Community is still heavily dependent upon imports from the rest of the world—petroleum, mineral ores, fuel, and (to a less extent) foodstuffs. No doubt, domestic substitutes for some of these inputs can be developed, but the Nine must still maintain an export trade that will earn an ample supply of foreign exchange. Failing that, they will be unable to enjoy either plenty or stability, and prospects for a just and efficient European economy may be hard to sustain. In that case, the European Community will at best become a hollow shell, at worst the corpse of a noble effort.

**SUGGESTED READINGS**

Andrew Shonfield, *Europe: Journey to an Unknown Destination* (London: Allan Lane, 1973).

>A nontechnical, thoughtful evaluation of the European Community's past, present, and future.

Charles Kindleberger, *Europe's Postwar Growth: The Role of Labor Supply* (Cambridge, Mass.: Harvard University Press, 1967).

>A specific interpretation of national rates of output growth in Western Europe during the 1950s and early 1960s.

Edward F. Denison, *Why Growth Rates Differ: Postwar Experience in Nine Western Countries* (Washington, D.C.: The Brookings Institution, 1967).

>A comprehensive econometric analysis of differential growth rates that supports but goes beyond Kindleberger's thesis.

# UNITED STATES
# OF AMERICA

7

We come, finally, to the economy of the United States of America. It is predominantly a market system, departing less than most others from the principles of economic individualism. Although a mature economy—some call it "post-industrial"—it is still the most productive on earth. It has been growing steadily, even if at times sedately. It performs reasonably well—providing freedom and plenty, maintaining a moderate degree of stability, and struggling to achieve equity. Yet it still has numerous problems to solve.

## THE ECONOMY'S ORGANIZATION

The decisions that govern economic activity in the United States are made mainly by individuals and small groups, widely scattered, relatively limited in scope, and coordinated through the mechanism of the market. But many of the more important decisions are made by giant corporations and, to a lesser extent, by labor unions. These institutions are highly concentrated, affect a broad segment of total economic activity, and are significantly insulated from the dictates of the market. Economic activity is also influenced to an increasing degree by governmental decisions, which reflect not market imperatives but the purposes of politics. The economy of the United States is thus a mixture of individualism and collectivism, like the separate and combined economies of Western Europe. In this mixture individualism is dominant, even more than it is on the Continent. But the component of collectivism in the United States deserves analysis as both an essential support and a potential danger to the market system.

**The business sector** At first glance, the American business system appears to be a direct descendant of the one described by Adam Smith in 1776. There are more than 10 million legally autonomous enterprises in the business population, most of them comparatively small (99.1 percent have fewer than 100 employees), most selling one or a few products or services, and most vigorously competing with others on the basis of price and quality. Entry of new firms into local markets is easy, and exit from the market is common and frequent.

The appearance is deceiving, because as nearly everyone knows, the great bulk of the nation's productive assets and the income they generate belongs to a small group of corporate giants whose reach extends into practically all corners of the economy. A mere 500 companies, including such well-known concerns as General Motors, Exxon, IBM, U.S. Steel, and RCA, produce nearly 70 percent of the nation's total industrial output. The largest 50 of the 500 enjoy a combined sales revenue of nearly $350 billion a year, a sum that approaches one-fourth of America's gross national product. General Motors alone employs nearly 60,000 workers and its yearly sales revenue exceeds $35 billion, more than the GNP of such countries as the Union of South Africa, Denmark, Austria, Yugoslavia, Turkey, and Norway.

To a certain extent, the two segments of the business system function independently of each other, the small firms competing among themselves and the giants doing the same. An undetermined but sizable number of small concerns each year loses its independence, however, through either mergers or quasi-mergers with great enterprises. Those whose assets are formally acquired become, of course, outright subsidiaries of the giants. Many more are subsidiaries in all but name: Some hold franchises or dealerships that transform them for practical purposes into agents of the great corporations; others are tightly bound by subcontracts or reciprocal buying agreements.

The upshot is that, while price and product competition persist throughout the American economy, the rivalry is increasingly among the few rather than the many. In other words, although the giant concerns have actual and potential rivals and thus are exposed in some degree to market forces, they can and do behave differently than the atomistic price-takers pictured in the model of economic individualism. The corporate giants have considerable discretion, for instance, in deciding what goods and services to produce, the quality of the products, their selling prices. And they have the resources to enter a wide variety of productive activities, to operate many different plants in many places at home and abroad, to decide where new plants are to be opened and others closed. The managers of the giant enterprises, in short, partially supplant the pricing mechanism in the allocation of resources in the United States and thus constitute centers of substantial economic power.

**The labor sector**   Some 94 million men and women are in the U.S. labor force, defined as all those of working age who are employed gainfully or actively seeking paid employment. Although entrance into many occupations is partially closed by educational, experiential, or licensure requirements, workers enjoy a very large degree of freedom of occupational choice, moving into and from occupations and specific jobs in accordance with their personal preferences with respect to pay, working conditions, geographic location, and so forth. Economic individualism is the rule, not the exception, in the allocation of labor resources in the United States.

To a considerable extent, wage rates (the prices of labor) are determined by the interplay of market forces. But both the demand for and supply of labor are significantly influenced by institutional factors, chiefly labor unions. Only 24 million workers, roughly 27 percent of the nation's nonfarm labor force, are organized, but unionism is firmly established in most of the major manufacturing, transportation, and communications industries, and it is expanding steadily in the services and governmental sectors of the economy, which now employ more than 60 percent of all American workers. Labor leaders in areas such as these have considerable power over workers, partially controlling their access to jobs and influencing their wages and working conditions. They also have substantial power over employers: by withholding the supply of labor, unions can raise wage rates or keep them from falling, change working conditions, and influence the level and composition of product demand. And unions have power over consumers, in that strikes reduce or cut off the supply of goods and services and union-caused increases in production and distribution costs often result in higher retail prices. In short, collective bargaining, especially when industrywide, can and often does distort the pricing mechanism as it allocates society's resources and distributes income.

**The governmental sector**    Although the American economy has been and continues to be governed primarily by market forces, it has never been a *laissez-faire* system in the full sense of the term. Private corporations have been regulated, to a greater or lesser extent, since the early days of the Republic. Federal, state, and local governments have for many years organized and operated business enterprises with monopoly power; the Postal Service, Tennessee Valley Authority, state liquor stores, and municipal power and water companies are examples. For nearly a century the Federal and many state governments have enforced the antitrust statutes against private enterprises with significant market power and have regulated the prices, output, and investment of various firms in industries with one or very few sellers—notably communications, transportation, and electric power. Since the early years of the twentieth century, the Federal government has used its authority to tax, spend, and create money to influence the rate of economic activity and alter the distribution of income. And initially in wartime, later in periods when the nation was not at war but was suffering unacceptably high rates of price inflation, the Federal government has tried to enforce an "incomes policy"— direct control over prices and wage rates in most, though not all, sectors of the economy.

Compared to most of the world's industrialized economies, the United States is still guided much more by individuals' than government's decisions. No less important to note is that whereas elsewhere social control of economic activity has evolved from a conviction that it will produce a more nearly optimal allocation of resources, greater stability, a higher rate of growth, and greater equity than will *laissez-faire*, in the United States governmental intervention has developed in small steps, each justified on the ground that it was necessary to preserve the market system. The Sherman Antitrust Act of 1890 and subsequent amendments were enacted to prevent reduction of competition; regulation by commission was instituted to protect consumers against predatory behavior by "natural monopolies"; compensatory fiscal and monetary policies were adopted to stabilize fluctuations in private spending that otherwise culminate in deep depressions or rampant inflation.

It is impossible to capture in a single statistic the nature and extent of governmental intervention in the American economy. For that reason we must examine briefly each of the major means by which governmental activity makes itself felt: public enterprises; taxes, purchases of goods and services, and transfer payments; money and credit; and direct regulation.

**Public enterprise**   Including public authorities and special districts, there are about 18,000 public enterprises in the United States. Most are local or regional in scope, but a few operate nationwide. Although none of the latter rivals the nation's largest corporations in sales or asset holdings, a few—like the Tennessee Valley Authority, Port of New York Authority, and the U.S. Postal Service—are custodians of many millions of dollars. Even so, public enterprises as a group carry little economic weight, accounting for only a fraction more than 1 percent of GNP and employing less than 2 percent of the nation's workers.

**Taxes, purchases, transfer payments**   Nearly one-third of the gross national product in the United States is taken in taxes by Federal, state, and local governments. Of this amount about one-third is returned in transfer payments: social insurance and welfare benefits, veterans' benefits, subsidies to private enterprises, and interest on the national debt. The remaining two-thirds is used to buy goods and services: military personnel and supplies, police and fire protection, educational supplies and services.

Because taxation reduces the disposable income of consumers and business concerns, it affects the level and distribution of income and the allocation of resources. The extent of its influence depends considerably upon the form the tax takes. Some levies, like the American income tax, are progressive: the ratio of tax to income rises as income rises. Others, such as the property tax and a general sales tax, are regressive: the tax/income ratio falls as income rises. According to two careful students of the problem, the combination of taxes now levied by all levels of government in the United States "is essentially proportional for the vast majority of families and therefore has little effect on the distribution of income."[1] In other words, the tax-rate structure gives most income receivers about the same voice in the allocation of productive resources.

Purchases of goods and services by the Federal, state, and local governments currently account for about one-fourth of the GNP;

[1] Joseph A. Pechman and Benjamin Okner, *Who Bears the Tax Burden?* (Washington, D.C.: The Brookings Institution, 1974), p. 10.

in 1929, by contrast, the fraction was only one-tenth. Sovereignty over this fourth of output and the resources employed to produce it lies not with individual consumers expressing their preferences in the marketplace, but with voters or their elected representatives. Nearly all the goods and services in question *must* be produced by government and paid for with tax revenues. The benefits of a military establishment, school system, police force, and so forth are enjoyed by everyone in society, and they cannot be subdivided so that each citizen is able to buy at a price exactly the amount of each that he or she wishes. In the quarter of the economy that falls within the governmental sector, collectivism is and largely has to be the rule.

Governments also affect the patterns of income distribution and resource allocation through payments to individuals, groups, and institutions, that are not currently providing productive services in return. Amounting to about 10 percent of GNP, these transfer payments include veterans benefits, old-age pensions, public assistance (welfare) benefits, subsidies to merchant shipping and airlines, educational opportunity grants, rent supplements, tax credits, and agricultural subsidies. The payments are often made in kind rather than in cash; for example, health care services provided without charge or at a price below cost of supply. And some subsidies are paid not by the taxpayer but by consumers, as is the case when foreign goods are excluded from the U.S. market by imposition of a tariff or quota.

The redistributive impact of specific subsidies on those who receive them is obvious. As to allocative effects, when a subsidy is financed by taxpayers, the subsidized product is sold at a price below its cost of supply. As a result, more of the nation's resources are devoted to its production, and less to the production of other things, than consumers would otherwise choose. When a subsidy is paid by consumers of the product, the price is well above cost. The result is that fewer resources are devoted to its production, and more resources to other goods, than consumers would choose.

**Regulation** Direct government intervention in American economic life takes many forms. In a small but growing number of areas, private consumption is subjected to public control. Efforts are made to prevent consumers from buying narcotics, viewing pornographic motion pictures, and (with exceptions) gambling. In the interest of personal health and safety, consumers are required to equip their cars with restraining belts, forgo consumption of certain products suspected of causing cancer, and get prescriptions for medicines previously sold over the counter. All these measures clearly interfere with freedom of consumers' choice and thus affect the allocation of resources.

Governmental regulation of specific kinds of business has also increased over the years. Firms in lines of production where there are significant economies of scale, such as electric power, telecommunications, and rail transport, are subjected to control by statutory commissions with authority to set maximum prices and standards for service. State and local boards and commissions also regulate prices, wage rates, or working conditions—and often all of these—of establishments selling milk, haircuts, health care, insurance, real estate, banking, and mortuary services.

General or economy-wide public regulation of prices and wage rates has been undertaken in the United States on several occasions in recent decades. In 1933–35, during the Great Depression, the National Recovery Administration attempted to manage a system of price and wage floors, developed through industry-wide "codes." In 1943–46, at the height of American participation in World War II, ceilings were imposed upon prices of virtually all goods and services, together with rationing arrangements for gasoline, tires, and key foods. A comparable, but less rigorous, system of general price and wage controls, without rationing, was instituted in 1951–52 while the nation was engaged in the Korean War. From 1962 to 1968, without explicit approval of the Congress, the Kennedy and Johnson Administrations conducted a campaign to restrain price and wage inflation in key sectors of the economy through a combination of exhortation and the manipulation of governmental stockpiles of goods. And from 1971 to 1974, beginning with a three-month "freeze" of prices and wage rates and followed by periods of varying degrees of restriction, the Nixon Administration tried to enforce an "incomes policy."

**Predominantly a market economy**   Despite its large and growing admixture of collectivism, the economy of the United States remains predominantly individualistic. Most of the demand for goods and services originates with individual consumers in a population of over 213 million. These decisions are shaped by advertising, salesmanship, and more subtle forms of cultural conditioning, but consumers have a wide degree of freedom in choosing among an immense variety of products and services. These outputs in turn reflect the efforts of several million individual enterprises, all established through private initiative and all privately owned and directed. Within broad limits, they are free to decide what they wish to produce, what method of production they will adopt, and how much to bid for the services of capital and labor. Income-receivers throughout the land are free to spend or save, and those who save are free to invest where they choose. Workers, too, have substantial freedom of occupational choice as well as high geographic mobility.

None of these persons, be they consumers, managers, investors, or workers, is subject to the dictates of an authoritarian control plan. Nearly all are subject in some measure to the discipline of the market. The economy of the United States may be mixed, or perhaps you prefer to call it mixed up, but it is still primarily a market economy.

## UNITED STATES DEVELOPMENT IN PERSPECTIVE

The long story of U.S. growth, with all its dangers and drama, has been one of great good fortune. Millions of people have improved their lot, some enormously and some very little, as growth varied from decade to decade and region to region. Even World Wars I and II, so damaging elsewhere, stimulated the U.S. economy. A post-industrial stage of development is now presenting new challenges.

**The fortunate Americans**   Compared to China and India, the United States has been able to develop without the constraints imposed by strong, rigid, premodern traditions. After pushing the American Indians aside, settlers could literally start from scratch. Looking back, one can see how many of the key elements in development were present in unusually favorable degree. Those who chose to come to the United States were venturesome and flexible; their innovative attitudes were expected and rewarded. Abundant arable land, forests, water, and minerals were seized without major resistance and exploited with comparative ease. A large volume of foreign investment for several decades assisted the early growth of the stock of fixed capital plant and equipment; on several occasions European investors found they had made unintended capital grants when bankruptcy erased their claims.

If U.S. growth, with all these advantages, has been fairly slow and frequently irregular, one can see by contrast why today's developing countries find it hard to make rapid, steady progress. Economic development has flourished in those parts of the world where conditions were most favorable; now the most difficult cases remain to be tackled.

**Income inequalities, personal and regional**   Over the last two centuries, U.S. citizens have on the whole been better off than their parents, have improved their own lot, and have expected their children to move beyond them. These gains have, however, by no means been equal for everyone. All during the nineteenth century, in particular, the range of incomes from lowest to highest appears to have widened as individuals at the upper end built huge fortunes by capitalizing on abundant opportunities, while wave after wave of immigrants came in to start at the bottom, where the nonwhite minority remained trapped. Although a great many immigrants and their heirs improved their position with time, the overall distribution of income became very unequal.

There were regional inequalities, too. Differences in average per capital income among regions have displayed a changing pattern over two centuries, reflecting unplanned responses to changing economic circumstances. But industries and regions with emerging opportunities have attracted migrants, thus tending to reduce interregional differences. Over the last half century, in particular, depressed regions have tended to come up closer to the national average.

**Stimulus of military expenditures**   Great Britain, France, Russia, and Germany all suffered major losses in men and capital during the first World War, whereas the United States emerged at the end of hostilities in a commanding economic position, in both absolute and relative terms. Although the other powers recovered during the interwar period, the second World War again saw relative and absolute U.S. gains. World War II imposed huge manpower and capital losses in the USSR, Germany, France, Great Britain and Japan, but the war cleared the ground for new physical capital and new institutions in these societies. By contrast, it revived the U.S. economy from a decade of depression and stimulated a new era of technological progress and economic growth.

At present, national security outlays absorb about 6 percent of the GNP in both the United States and the USSR, in part fueling research and development efforts that have some spillover into civilian activities, more so in the United States than in the Soviet Union. Military outlays raise income and employment in almost every Congressional district and are hard to challenge politically. Veterans' benefits make up a significant fraction of the transfer programs that constitute our welfare state. If the major powers could agree on mutual reductions in military outlays, resources could no doubt be shifted to other uses, perhaps to economic development programs. Beating swords into plowshares is not economically impossible; it is, however, politically difficult. United States military outlays dropped from $336 billion to $27 billion (in 1974 prices) between 1944 and 1947 as the United States converted to peace after World War II; from 1969 to 1971 as the United States extricated itself from Indochina, the fall was from $120 billion to $92 billion.[2]

**Post-industrial pioneering**  Since World War II, more than half the U.S. labor force has been engaged, not in agriculture and manufacturing, but in producing services. Table 7-1 shows trends from 1929 to 1974; the first column portrays the steady rise in services employment, both in absolute numbers and as a share of the labor force. Almost two-thirds of the labor force is now earning a living through providing a vast variety of useful services: fighting fires, selling stocks, piloting aircraft, nursing, providing legal counsel, typing, teaching college. Modern technology has made U.S. farms so productive that 4 percent of the labor force now supplies more than our doctors want us to eat. Labor-saving technology and abundant capital have made manufacturing workers so productive that commodity production outside agriculture engages only a third of the labor force. But because services activity involves the complexities of human behavior, it creates new problems of management for efficiency and equity.

2 These are rough figures in 1974 dollars, obtained by using the 1958-base implicit price deflator for all Federal purchases of goods and services.

## TABLE 7-1
## Composition of the U.S. Labor Force, Selected Years, 1929–1974 (in thousands)

|  | SERVICES[a] | MANUFAC-TURING[b] | AGRI-CULTURE[c] | UNEMPLOYED | TOTAL |
|---|---|---|---|---|---|
| 1929 | 24,154 | 13,286 | 10,450 | 1,550 | 49,440 |
| 1939 | 24,228 | 12,282 | 9,610 | 9,480 | 55,600 |
| 1949 | 34,074 | 17,536 | 7,656 | 3,637 | 62,903 |
| 1959 | 41,249 | 20,367 | 5,565 | 3,740 | 70,921 |
| 1969 | 53,491 | 24,311 | 3,606 | 2,832 | 84,240 |
| 1974 | 59,999 | 24,673 | 3,492 | 5,076 | 93,240 |
| **Percent Shares** | | | | | |
| 1929 | 48.9 | 26.9 | 21.1 | 3.1 | 100.0 |
| 1939 | 43.6 | 22.1 | 17.3 | 17.0 | 100.0 |
| 1949 | 54.1 | 27.9 | 12.2 | 5.8 | 100.0 |
| 1959 | 58.2 | 28.7 | 7.8 | 5.3 | 100.0 |
| 1969 | 63.5 | 28.8 | 4.3 | 3.4 | 100.0 |
| 1974 | 64.4 | 26.5 | 3.7 | 5.4 | 100.0 |

[a] Wholesale and retail trade; government; services; transportation and public utilities; finance, insurance, and real estate; armed forces; nonagricultural self-employed.
[b] Manufacturing, mining, and contract construction.
[c] Agriculture, forestry, and fisheries.

SOURCE: Rearranged from date in Tables C-24 and C-29, *Economic Report of the President* (February 1975), pp. 276 and 282.

There are several reasons for the shift from the production of goods to the provision of services. Mass production by large specialized centers calls for a greater expenditure of effort on distribution; large-scale enterprise requires more effort in finance; and urbanization requires more effort in government. But these are not the only reasons. The fact is that the American economy is now producing not only more food than we need, but more goods of many kinds than consumers voluntarily demand. An increasing amount of effort must be devoted to advertising and salesmanship to persuade us to buy them. The surfeit of goods also permits us to spend more money on personal services including entertainment, recreation, and travel.

# INTERACTING UNITED STATES GROWTH RATES

The growth of output and population in the United States, together with expansion of the capital stock and a sustained rise in the level of technology, have involved complex influences and changing relationships. Careful review of their main features suggests both the sources of past progress and the areas where remedies for present problems may be found.

**Population trends**    The population of the United States grew before World War I from 3.9 million in 1790 to 100.5 million in 1915, at an average rate of 2.63 percent per year. At first, in the predominantly young population, the birth rate was remarkably high—52 per thousand in 1820! During the nineteenth century it fell gradually; by 1920 it was 28 per thousand total population. The death rate fell over the same period from 23 to 13. In addition, there was a huge flow of immigrants: around 10,000 annually in the 1820s, 100,000 in the early 1840s, 500,000 around 1885, and a million per year around 1910. A continent was being filled, added population was welcome, and today's concern over population pressure simply did not exist.

Over the last 60 years, U.S. population has grown from 100.5 million in 1915 to 213.4 million in 1975, at an average rate of 1.52 percent per year. The birth rate dropped from 28 per thousand total population in 1920 to 19 in the 1930s, rose to 25 in the 1950s, and dropped to 15 in the early 1970s. Death rates trended downward over the same period from 13 to 9 per thousand. Legislation restricted immigration, which fell to the level of 500,000 annually in the 1920s, dropped sharply to 50,000 per year in the 1930s, rose to 300,000 in the 1950s, and has averaged 400,000 per year during 1967–75.

The proportion of the population between ages 16 and 65 that is at work or looking for work (the "participation rate") was 56 percent in 1940, rose to 63.1 percent in 1944, fell back to 57.2 percent in 1946, and has gradually drifted up to 61.8 percent in 1974, reflecting chiefly the greater participation of women in the labor force. Average hours worked per week have come down from 43 in 1940 to about 37 today. While the shorter work week tended to reduce labor input, the effect was roughly offset by qualitative improvement in labor as measured by the worker's educational attainment.

**Making labor more productive**  Labor input growth only accounts for about 29 percent of total output expansion in the United States over the 1929–69 period.[3] The most important additional factor has been advances in knowledge (technological, managerial, and organizational), accounting for about 31 percent of output growth. A wide variety of innovations, difficult to disentangle and hard to measure, have proved to be the most powerful engine of progress around us. Additional capital has helped, especially since World War II, and increased education per worker has also been important. The shift of people out of agriculture and small-scale self-employment into better-paying occupations accounts for 10 percent of output growth over this period. These forces act jointly; advances in knowledge get embodied in new capital and in better-trained labor, all brought to bear in expanding sectors of the economy. Taken by itself, mere capital expansion would have modest results, just as greater labor input without these associated changes would quickly confront diminishing returns. The key point is that, in all this interaction, more than half the overall growth came from more effective use of inputs, less than half from merely adding more labor, capital, and land.

## THE ECONOMY'S PERFORMANCE

Compared to the other economies we have examined, and compared to earlier periods in United States history, the post-1945 U.S. economy has clearly performed remarkably well in most respects. Applying the same tests used in earlier chapters, we offer brief comments on strong and weak points under each heading. Can the areas of strong performance be extended, and can the points of weakness be repaired?

**Economic plenty**  Thanks in large part to its flexible market system, the U.S. economy provides an annual flow of goods and services that is truly abundant. Most people are amply fed, so much so that weight control has become a thriving industry.

[3] See Edward F. Denison, *Accounting for United States Economic Growth, 1929–1969* (Washington, D.C.: The Brookings Institution, 1974), especially Chapter 9, pp. 124–50.

Attractive and low-cost clothing has been a notable United States contribution to international progress. Nine out of ten U.S. families live in dwelling units with inside plumbing, hot and cold running water, electric lighting, and adequate heat—fundamentals still lacking for most of the world's population. Of 63 million households in 1970, 47 million were living in single-family houses, of which 40 million were owner-occupied. Eighty-two percent of all homes had telephones, and 95 percent had refrigerators. The U.S. stock of housing is so ample that old or badly located units are simply abandoned, whereas in other societies they would be eagerly repaired.

The U.S. standard of living now goes far beyond these basic needs. Education is generously provided: Of all persons 25 years or older in 1973, 13 percent had completed four years of college, 60 percent had completed twelve years of grade school and high school, 76 percent had completed eight years of grade school; only 4.5 percent had received less than five years of schooling. The level of health care, hard to measure, is for all but the poorest families rarely equaled elsewhere and certainly far above what the bulk of the world's population receives. United States consumers have the time and the income for a wide diversity of recreation, entertainment, and leisure-time activities. Of all households, 98 percent have TV sets; 82 percent have at least one automobile, and nearly a third have two or more cars. The average U.S. citizen, including babes in arms, traveled over 6,200 miles in 1972 (87 percent of this by passenger automobile), a degree of individual mobility unequaled in human history.

Critics of the economy complain that too much is spent on consumer goods that are luxurious, even frivolous; too little on essential social services. Vehicles weighing more than two tons, furnished with softly upholstered couches and driven with the power of 300 horses, carry people in air-conditioned ease, one by one, along the highways. Trivial gifts, elaborately packaged, are exchanged on holidays and anniversaries, their cost running to more than a billion dollars a year. At the same time, essential public services provided by police and fire departments, hospitals, and schools, to say nothing of libraries, museums, parks, and zoos, are cut back for lack of funds. Moreover, it is now obvious that in creating material abundance the U.S. economy also produces dangerous and unpleasant damage to the environment—bads rather than goods, subverting some of our apparent plenty.

These faults have several causes; there may be several remedies. John Kenneth Galbraith blames the power of large corporations and their influence on the government. For him, the remedy lies in an informed public and a more independent House of Representatives.[4] Underfinancing of municipal government services reflects a genuine dilemma in economic organization: How should the necessary costs of these basic services be covered? New principles and new channels for collecting public revenue may be required. Sharply increased costs and prices may alter buying patterns: The large American automobile may be doomed. Legislative standards and taxes on pollutants can reach other aspects of these problems.

**Economic freedom** When demand is slack in the United States, access to a job is limited. In some occupations—for example, the building trades—access is informally limited by ethnic barriers, while in other occupations it is artificially constrained—for example, among morticians—by legally sanctioned monopoly restrictions. Nevertheless, compared with most other economies, the United States offers a wide range of employment opportunities, thus opening an upward road for millions. Freedom of geographic movement is greater than in any of the other economies we have examined. Whether the attraction has been job opportunities, a more pleasant climate, or larger welfare payments, millions of families have moved from one part of the United States to another without hindrance. Finally, though not least, the market mechanism makes available a far greater diversity of goods and services than anywhere else in the world.

**Economic justice** The extreme income inequalities of the past are substantially smaller today, as can be seen from the data in Table 7-2. Where half a century ago the top 5 percent of U.S. families received 30 percent of the personal income, in 1971 their share was 19.1 percent. The lowest 20 percent of U.S. families received 3.5 percent of all personal income in 1929; this fraction was 4.8 percent in 1971. Property income is a far smaller share of the total now than in the past, and transfer payments are far larger. But most of this change had taken place by the mid-1940s, and

[4] See John K. Galbraith, *Economics and the Public Purpose* (Boston: Houghton Mifflin, 1973).

since then the share of the lowest fifth has not increased at all. The relative gains have come to the middle 60 percent of the income distribution, those with 1974 incomes (after tax) running roughly $7,500 to $19,000. Those in the bottom fifth, although much better off in real terms than fifty years ago, are as far below the national median now as they were then.

Sixteen million out of the 25 million U.S. citizens with 1972 incomes below the officially determined poverty level were white. The other 9 million (36 percent of the total) were made up of black, Chicano, native American, and Puerto Rican minorities, who together constitute only 13 percent of the population. This over-representation of racial minorities at the low end of the income structure reflects, among other things, a long era of systematic discrimination in education, housing, and jobs. The mid-1975 unemployment rate for whites was 8.0 percent; for other groups, 14.2 percent. Life expectancy at birth is 72.1 years for whites and 65.5 years for others. In 1972, the median income of white families was $11,500; for others it was $7,100. Thus, in spite of legislation and substantial effort, the inequities of the past have not yet been eliminated.

An initial drive on these problems was launched in 1964 with President Johnson's "war on poverty." Over the next six years, more than $10 billion of federal funds was spent on a variety of job-training, social service, and community action programs, all designed to improve the income-earning abilities of the able-bodied poor and to give the young, the old, the sick and disabled

**TABLE 7-2**

**Percent Shares of U.S. Households in Personnel Income, Selected Years, 1929–72**

|                    | 1929 | 1941 | 1947 | 1961 | 1971 |
|--------------------|------|------|------|------|------|
| Top 5 percent      | 30.0 | 24.0 | 20.9 | 19.6 | 19.1 |
| Next 15 percent    | 24.4 | 24.8 | 25.1 | 25.9 | 25.6 |
| Middle 60 percent  | 42.1 | 47.1 | 49.0 | 49.9 | 50.5 |
| Lowest 20 percent  | 3.5  | 4.1  | 5.0  | 4.6  | 4.8  |

SOURCE: Daniel B. Radner and John C. Hinrichs, "Size Distribution of Income in 1964, 1970, and 1971," *Survey of Current Business*, Oct. 1974, p. 27.

enough purchasing power to maintain at least a minimal level of decency. Although large in absolute amount, the outlays were tiny compared to the size and severity of the problems, leading many observers to assert that the war was not lost but rather was never seriously fought. In any case, beginning in 1969 the nation's antipoverty efforts were switched to a different strategy, one that called for putting "floors" under income through guaranteed payments rather than opening "doors" to greater economic opportunity.

A "floors" policy could meet the problem of inadequate incomes if the guaranteed minimum were high enough to enable low-income families to cover their major unmet needs. The necessary figure is estimated to be roughly twice the official poverty threshhold of about $4,400 per year for a family of four in 1974. At present, however, the voting public does not seem ready to endorse negative taxation on this scale. Resistance is strongest among those who are not far above the poverty line themselves. Economists and legislators thus face a major task in trying to develop a workable set of taxes and transfers that will raise all incomes to a decent level while preserving what appear to the American people to be reasonable differentials.

**Stability and security**     Until the last quarter century, the most serious defect of the US economy was its price and output instability. Periodically, business was plunged into deep depressions; plants shut down, firms went into bankruptcy, the stock market crashed, banks closed their doors, investors lost their savings, and people lost their jobs. Many months might pass before activity revived. Business instability caused personal insecurity. Men could not count on their jobs, the safety of their savings, or the solvency of their enterprises.

Since World War II, lapses from full employment have been much smaller, and until recently the upward drift of prices has been modest. Fiscal and monetary policy have been used to reduce fluctuations in the private sector. Bank deposits and other forms of savings are now insured. The ups and downs of the stock market have less impact on the whole economy than they used to, and trading practices are more closely supervised. For all but a disadvantaged minority, employment is steadier, and if it stops, unemployment insurance provides temporary support. Business still fluctuates, but the swings are moderate compared to those of the

Drawing by Geo. Price; © 1974 The New Yorker Magazine, Inc.

past. A more serious danger now lies in a chronic combination of painful unemployment and serious inflation.

Although upward and downward swings in United States economic activity are now moderate compared to those of the past, they remain troublesome. Of special concern is the fact that there have been several periods when painfully high unemployment rates coincided with general price inflation. The most serious came in 1974–75 when the unemployment rate hit a peak of over 9 percent while the consumer price index was rising at more than 9 percent per year. Real output fell roughly 6 percent from the 1973 peak, as efforts to limit inflation took priority over efforts to sustain output and employment.

The United States was slower to develop social insurance programs than most other developed economies, but social security and other support programs were launched under the New Deal in the 1930s. Since World War II the programs have been extended with bipartisan support, and since the mid-1960s they have rapidly increased their share of all government spending. In fiscal 1965, transfer payments by Federal, state, and local governments totaled $35 billion, while national security outlays were $49 billion. Ten years later, in fiscal 1975, total transfer payments reached $155 billion while national security outlays were $85 billion. This huge expansion in welfare payments covers social security, old age assistance, health programs and many others.

---

**FIG. 7-1**
**General Price Level Indexes, Six Economies,**
**1952–75, by Year (1952 = 100)**

---

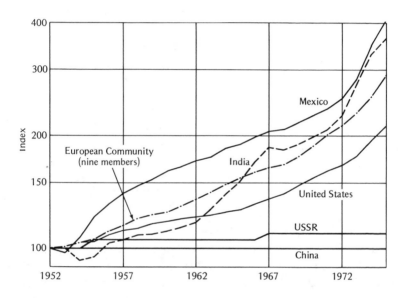

SOURCES: These gross domestic product deflators measure the difference between GDP in current prices and GDP in constant prices, relative to a base year. They are transcribed or computed from data in United Nations, *Yearbook of National Accounts Statistics*, various years; Statistical Office of the European Community, *National Accounts Aggregates*, various years; and Government of India, Central Statistical Office, *Estimates of National Product*, various years, supplemented by preliminary estimates for 1974 and 1975 as noted in individual chapters above. The crude estimate for the USSR shows a 5 percent rise in 1955 and another 5 percent rise in 1967, years when most government-fixed prices were raised by roughly this percentage. In the absence of any statistical evidence, the line for China records an assertedly unchanged price level.

---

The rise of U.S. money incomes since World War II has been partly offset by a rising cost of living, but until recently the rate of inflation was modest. As Figure 7-1 shows, the U.S. record of price stability has been better than that of the nine-member European Community, India, and Mexico. A general price index for the United States in 1975 stood at 212 (1952 = 100); the Mexican index was 404; India's, 362; and the European Community's, 288. The USSR and China, on the other hand, show up more favorably in this comparison, since price level increases have been suppressed through rigid controls in the USSR and controls plus rationing in China. The upward drift of prices in the United States and the European Community has quickened since the mid-1960s, and since 1973 the upward spurt has been alarming in most parts of the world.

**Economic growth** Throughout this book, growth has been stressed as an important economic objective. Low-income countries try to increase their output because their population is growing and their people are poor. Middle-income countries may have less population pressure but may want to catch up with the rich and powerful. Why, however, should the United States, a superpower with almost the highest per capita income in the world, seek to grow still more? Do the costs of further growth now outweigh its benefits?

The potential for growth continues to lie both in applying new knowledge effectively and in a larger flow of inputs. Innovations in products, processes, and institutional arrangements seem to come forward as rapidly now as at any time in the last 200 years, and as these innovations are put to use they permit either more output, more voluntary leisure, or more unemployment. The U.S. population continues to expand absolutely, even though birth rates are falling, and the total will continue to grow for several more decades. Current savings and investment are on a massive scale, and new outlets for them must continually be found. On the supply side, therefore, pressure to take advantage of opportunities for enlarging the national product creates its own argument for growth.

Further pressure for progress comes from the stern logic of long-run international economic relations. In a world of countries vigorously diversifying and modernizing their economies, the nation that is content to stand still must soon fall behind. For in short order it will find itself burdened with outdated skills, plants, and machinery. Its share of the world's export markets will decline, even as its demand for cheaper and better import rises. The resulting balance-of-payments difficulties, as America's recent experience strongly attests, will inevitably compound and be compounded by adverse movements in prices, wages, national income, and employment at home. In short, for healthy survival in the highly competitive modern world, an economy must progress—and progress rapidly enough to keep up with its potentialities.

In the past, output growth has, however, been overencouraged because its full costs have been ignored. By leaving out the costs of damage to our environment, producers have been able to offer us goods and services at understated prices, thus failing to warn us of their full costs. The remedy for environment-damaging output expansion lies, of course, in building full costs into the price of the output; consumers will then voluntarily cut their consumption back to what they "really" want, and the sums they pay will finance repairs to the environment. Large amounts are now being spent on research and development to find innovations that will reduce the environmental damage caused by modern agriculture, mining, and manufacturing; as new methods gradually emerge, commodity production can expand without the present level of harm to the environment. It is nevertheless obvious that economic growth from now on will have to be more prudent than ever before if mankind is to survive.

**Elements of a U.S. agenda**    As the United States begins its third century of national independence, its citizens are confronted with the need to change dramatically many attitudes and forms of economic behavior. For one thing, the era of cheap energy is over and with it is ending a style of life that prominently features dependence upon private automobiles, spacious single-family homes with year-round climate control, and vast and varied consumption of relatively inexpensive products created from petrochemicals. Major, often wrenching, adjustments will be necessary in modes of production and consumption as steadily rising prices of energy compel conservation of fossil fuels. Some of the consequences will be distasteful, even painful, but not all: The yearly carnage on the highways will probably diminish sharply, as will the discharge of poisonous hydrocarbons into the air we breathe; large central cities may well regain their earlier appeal as places to live and work, thereby retarding or stopping the costly process of "urban sprawl"; the pace of life throughout the country may become less frantic, less damaging to physical and mental well-being.

Also coming to a close for U.S. citizens is the era of cheap and abundant foods and raw materials. Technological leadership, together with economic and military power, has until now enabled the United States to make lavish use of primary products imported from every corner of the world. But as other economies on all continents develop and grow themselves, they will be increasingly inclined to curb their exports of raw materials in favor of greater domestic consumption or form cartels to raise export prices, or both. In any case, U.S. imports of raw materials will become increasingly expensive and the U.S. share of world consumption may decline, forcing significant adjustments in the composition of total output and U.S. citizens' level of living. Again, however, the necessary adjustments may be in the end to our net benefit: We may be compelled to exploit our comparative advantage in agriculture and resume the role we played in the nineteenth century as the world's leading supplier of food and other farm products.

The history of the United States has been marked by a long series of institutional changes that have improved the economy's effectiveness. Further improvements are now required, particularly in the development of decentralized yet coordinated organs of economic management. Giant bureaucracies, both public and private, seem to perform less effectively than small or medium-sized units that take full advantage of modern information flows and data-processing methods. The market mechanism provides loose coordination and these smaller units respond alertly. Economic performance can be improved also through greater use of forecasting techniques and the employment of simulation procedures for pretesting new products, processes, and programs in the interest of minimizing unwanted second-order consequences.

Finally, we face disturbing issues of economic justice and equity, both among U.S. citizens and in relation to the millions of human beings in the poorest economies of the world today. At home the task is to enable all those groups that have lagged behind the majority to become more productive so they can share fully in the general abundance. Achievement of this goal will be especially difficult because it requires modification of beliefs and institutions that are deeply embedded in the nation's culture. And even if all groups in the U.S. economy achieve parity, there will still be the rest of the world to consider. Ultimately the fruits of knowledge and progress should enable all human beings to live productive lives in peace and dignity, as the development process reaches all peoples. What role can and should the United States play toward that end?

## SUGGESTED READINGS

Galbraith, John Kenneth, *Economics and the Public Purpose*. Boston: Houghton Mifflin, 1973.

> A major commentator restates his position.

Gordon, Robert Aaron, *Economic Instability and Growth: The American Record*. New York: Harper & Row, 1974.

> Informed review by a senior analyst.

Heilbroner, Robert L., *An Inquiry into the Human Prospect*. New York: W.W. Norton, 1974.

> An eloquent warning by an influential thinker.

North, Douglass C., *Growth and Welfare in the American Past*. Englewood Cliffs: Prentice-Hall, 1974 (2nd ed.).

> A very clear summary of U.S. economic history using recent evidence and new analytic methods.

Okun, Arthur M., *Equality and Efficiency: The Big Tradeoff*. Washington: Brookings Institution, 1975.

> Three thoughtful essays by a former member of the President's Council of Economic Advisors.

A
B 6
C 7
D 8
E 9
F 0
G 1
H 2
I 3
J 4